MADEIRA
AND
PORTO SANTO

BONECHI

© Copyright by Casa Editrice Bonechi - Florence - Italy
E-mail: bonechi@bonechi.it

Publication created by Casa Editrice Bonechi
Publication manager: Giovanna Magi
Photographic research, graphic design, layout and cover: Sonia Gottardo
Texts: Catanho Fernandes
Editing: Patrizia Fabbri
Translation: Cintra Tradutores CRL
Plan: Centro Studi Tecnici, Sesto Fiorentino, Firenze

Printed in Italy by Centro Stampa Editoriale Bonechi - Sesto Fiorentino

Photographs from the Casa Editrice Bonechi *Archives taken by* Luigi Di Giovine *and* Paolo Giambone.
Photographs pages 34 top, 35 top, middle and bottom left, 48-49, 51 top, 52 top, 59 bottom 66, 67, 68 top, 69 bottom,
70-71, 72, 100-101, 103, 110, 111, 112-113 : © Paulo Sotero.
Photograph pages 90-91: © Sie-Simephoto.

ISBN 978-88-476-1249-5
www.bonechi.com

* * *

Fishing boats and leisure craft moored at Paúl do Mar.

Introduction

*T*he Madeira archipelago comprises two principal islands - Madeira, from which it takes its name, and Porto Santo, the first land discovered by the Portuguese during the Voyages of Discovery and overseas colonisation, which began in the 15th century.

The Portuguese navigators first landed on Porto Santo, the 'golden island', in 1418. The following year, they set sail for Madeira and established the first captaincy in Machico, a sheltered bay fronting a deep, lush valley, sun-drenched and of exceptional beauty.

The capital of the archipelago is the city of Funchal, first settled in 1425, built on another attractive bay and enclosed by a natural amphitheatre rising from the sea to the mountains behind. The first city, according to the historians of the time, was built, as Gaspar Frutuoso relates, "in a beautiful valley, with curious trees and filled with fennel right down to the sea".

In addition to the two principal islands, the Autonomous Region of Madeira, the political and administrative designation created under the Constitution of the Portuguese Republic, includes the **Ilhas Desertas** (Deserted Islands) *and the* **Ilhas Selvagens** (Wilderness Islands), *which are uninhabited. The island of Madeira has an area of 741 square kilometres – 57 kilometres long and 22 kilometres wide. The total population is estimated at 260,000 inhabitants, of whom around 120,000 live in Funchal and neighbouring parishes.*

Now in the 21st century, the Archipelago of Madeira is an Autonomous Region with its own government with wide executive powers, and its own Parliament **(Assembleia Legislativa Regional)** ("Regional Legislative Assembly") with legislative powers. The population is mainly employed in the service sector, principally in tourism, the major source of the islands' income. The exquisite landscape, with its steep valleys and lush forests heavy with flowers, is typical of the island of Madeira, which combines these natural assets with an excellent climate and peace and quiet. The modernisation and building of new roads and hotels has transformed Madeira and Porto Santo into quality holiday destinations, attracting tourists all the year round from all over the world.

Geography and Environment

Madeira is characterised by its basalt rocks and pebble beaches, also made of basalt. The island is distinguished mainly, however, by its extremely varied but highly specific vegetation.

The Laurisilva Forest dates from the Tertiary Period of the Earth's history and once covered vast areas of Europe. It was one of the main victims of the last glaciations, surviving only in the geographical area of Macaronesia - Madeira, the Azores, the Canary Islands and Cape Verde. The forest reaches its greatest extent in Madeira, some 22,000 hectares, and it is here also that it contains the greatest variety of fauna and flora.

The most characteristic flora of the Laurisilva Forest include trees such as the til, the laurel, the Madeira mahogany, the ironwood, the whitewood, the lily-of-the-valley tree, the mock privet and the Canary laurel, in addition to shrubs and herbaceous plants, some of them unique to Madeira. Plants of medium height adding to the forest's diversity include the Madeira holly, the Canary holly, the mountain vine, the Madeira berberis and the fustic. Prominent among the shrubs and herbaceous plants are hawkweeds, daisies, brooms, everlasting flowers, mountain stocks, geraniums, moscardo orchids and several varieties of small orchids, including the extremely rare mountain orchid, unknown outside Madeira.

Occupying ground between 300 and 1300 metres, the Laurisilva forest performs a vital role in protecting the soil from erosion and encouraging rain water penetration. Recognised as a living relic, almost the whole of the area in which it occurs is included in the Madeira Nature Park, which has the highest protection status as a Total Reserve.

Banana plantations at
Câmara de Lobos.
Bunch of bananas.

Wine plantation in North Madeira.

Vegetation

Papaya tree.

*T*he cultivation of the banana and other tropical fruits, principally the custard apple and the papaya, is of major economic importance to the Autonomous Region of Madeira, as many families depend on them for their livelihoods.

Câmara de Lobos and the whole of the south coast of the island, especially Madalena do Mar are major banana growing areas. This crop is grown mainly in the warmer parts of the island, such as the entire coastline from Câmara de Lobos to Paúl do Mar. The banana tree produces only one crop per year, and new trees spring from the trunk, and only grow to maturity after the crop has been harvested and the old tree has been cut down.

Nowadays, younger farmers are beginning to use new technologies to lighten the work, such as sophisticated tools and machinery and trickle irrigation. In earlier days, it was the island farmer who, day after day, shaped the island's farmlands with toil and loving care.

The farmlands off the beaten track in the island's interior offer fascinating landscapes and contribute to the island's typical vegetation.

The Madeira regional authorities are attempting to persuade international organisations, particularly European ones, that banana growing should be protected, despite its poor economic return as a result of strong competition from Latin American countries, so as not to reduce further the attractive green patchwork that is a characteristic part of the Madeira landscape.

Grape production was first adopted by the villages in the north of the municipality of Câmara de Lobos, such as the parish of Estreito de Câmara de Lobos, where it was introduced in 1425. The vineyards are also partly responsible for the green in the landscape, contributing to the picturesque sight of tiny patches of cultivated land **"fajãs"** on the rock-walled terraces.

Flakes

*T*hanks to its sub-tropical climate, which is mild throughout the year, Madeira is an ideal place to grow flowers. Flowers, you could say, are the calling card of this island. In every corner, in public places and private areas there are gardens and a vast decorative display of plants, such as the bushes, which give the gardens and public areas a special style and familiar smell. Madeira nights have been quoted by poets, in songs and books, precisely because of that unforgettable perfume. Madeira has several municipal gardens, permanently well kept and where many multi-coloured species of flower delight the more romantic and nature-loving visitors. Characterised as a "Sea-side Garden", Madeira is sought after throughout the year by botanical groups and floriculturists, who come to Madeira to study.

The city of Funchal has won prizes over recent years, being awarded European prizes for the most flowery city, which has obviously added to its tourist appeal.

The Flower Festival takes place every year in spring, and attracts thousands of tourists. There is a great deal of commitment to this Festival, especially among the youth, and the island's schools. For this reason, the Festival has achieved success in only a few years, and has become one of the most important tourist events in Madeira. The island has flowers that are characteristic of several tropical countries, grown in the open air, as well as floriculture centres for intensive production, in which flowers are grown for decoration and export, which are also noteworthy. As well as the Botanical Garden in Funchal, where species are catalogued, with their respective origins, there are also private gardens where visitors can see the different stages of the growth of the flowers, and how they should be taken care of. It is also possible to buy flowers to take off the island, which are packaged in such a way as to last for several days. Generally, all of the estates on the island have their own gardens. The private gardens are decorated with flowerbeds, in amongst the grass lawns or miniature trees. A particularly noteworthy flower is the 'bird-of-paradise', a long-lasting flower characteristic of the tropical islands, as well as the anthurium, the protea, from the island itself and from South Africa, and a whole variety of season flowers which almost spontaneously shoot up all over the island. Flowers are a part of everyday living for the people of Madeira, and they are a fitting accompaniment to the welcoming and hospitable nature of the island and islander.

Right: Bird of paradise (Strelitzia regine ait).

Night heron (Callistemon rigidus R. Br.).

Vanda Coerulea Orchid.

Facing page: Cattleya Orchid (Cattleya sp.).

Wickerwork

Wickerwork developed into a craft industry from the middle of the 19th century. It is still made today in the small town of Camacha, one of the most picturesque in Madeira, not merely as a craft but also to preserve a tradition.

The craft is carried on as a home industry by men and women working on a piecework basis in between their domestic chores. The osiers are grown on well-watered or easily irrigated lands alongside streams or brooks, almost everywhere on the island. After cutting and drying in the sun, the canes are boiled in metal tanks over wood fires and the bark is then removed. Only after this are they worked. Before the arrival of competition from Asian countries, wickerwork was exported in large quantities to Europe, both light pieces and medium-weight and heavy pieces.

Light pieces include flower baskets and small decorative items; medium-weight pieces, baskets and boxes for domestic use; and heavy pieces, indoor and garden furniture.

Wickerwork has been part of Madeira life since the times of the first colonists.

It is less important nowadays but its production is still significant, both for farmers and for craftsmen working in small family co-operatives.

Lorry carrying dried wicker for working.

Stripping wicker after baking.

Pages 10-11:
Top, lorry carrying dried wicker for working and baking wicker after cutting; bottom, stripping wicker after baking and preparing wicker after stripping.

This page:
Wicker is harvested between January and March in the damp valleys of the North Coast. After being treated and dried in the sun it is selected according to thickness, the thickest canes generally used for furniture bases or large baskets.

Embroidery

*M*adeira embroidery is entirely hand-made. It has long been regarded in Europe and America as the prettiest embroidery in the world, appreciated by connoisseurs, especially the European royal houses. It was a British subject, a Miss Phelps, who brought the first Madeira embroidery to Victorian England in 1850. The embroideries made by the island's peasant women, at that time living virtually from subsistence agriculture, enchanted the English court and high society. It was richly worked with detail and finely made, and soon achieved prominence.

It has responded to various influences and has acquired its own identity by maintaining its characteristic design and exceptional delicacy and beauty. In Madeira, embroidery is worked on linen, natural silk, organdie, cambric and cotton. The stitches and designs vary according to the cloth and the purpose for which it is intended. Getting to know the names and techniques is also a way of discovering the history of Madeira: if we want to see what the Sunday shirts of well-off farm workers were like, we need to look

Cottage embroiderers. In rural areas these are often found working outside their houses.

for five tiny joined leaves in a single central knot known here as "widow's stitch". To embroider on organdie, we need to learn the techniques of the craft and of shadow work ... even the colours tell us about changing tastes and the differences from one village to another.

Nowadays, demand has fallen greatly. The embroideries are expensive and suffer from competition from other countries and machinery that produces very similar copies. For this reason, a seal of quality has been created to certify Madeira Embroidery made by the nimble hands of many Madeira women. It continues to be a living tradition passed down from generation to generation, made with an inimitable perfection that comes from long apprenticeship.

Traditions and Customs

*M*adeiran folklore is characterised by its lively music and colourful dances. A certain Moorish influence survives in a few of the slower songs, but generally it is an expression of celebration and enjoyment at traditional fairs and festivals.

Most people are familiar with the dance known as the **"bailinho"**. There is another, however, more popular and more rustic, called the **"brinco"** that country people play at traditional festivals, in which they sing and dance highly inventive sequences of steps. Completely without rules, the **"brinco"** is sung and danced by all, and no special costume is needed. Anybody who wants can join in the ring.

Despite the fact that the **"brinquinho"** (a percussion staff decorated with puppets and castanets) is a Madeiran instrument, it is only used in choreographed bailinho (this type of bailinho emerged when the first traditional song and dance groups began to appear about 50 years ago). It is these groups who nowadays perform the songs and dances of Madeira, and keep alive the traditional ballads sung by the chorus to the accompaniment of the **viola de arame** (bass guitar), the **rajão** (Madeiran guitar), the **braguinha** (ukelele), the fiddle, the harmonica, the tambourine, timbrels, bass drum, other percussion instruments and, more recently, the accordion.

Madeira Wine

Madeira wine is one of the archipelago's best-known products around the world. Historians believe that the first vines were introduced at the time of colonisation. The Jesuit fathers marketed the first wine and owned extensive vineyards. It was through the export of this full-bodied wine that the monastic order achieved great economic power and exercised its considerable social influence.

It was the English, however, who were responsible for the major growth of Madeira wine from the 18th century onwards, when their ships were in the habit of calling at the island en route to and from the West Indies. Madeira wine is made from the fermented juice of fresh grapes. The wine's dry or sweet palate depends on its residual sugar level.

The grapes from approved and recommended varieties, all of them European, are nowadays pressed mechanically in the wineries. In former days, they were trodden on by foot by farmers in traditional wine-presses on properties with larger vineyards and their own cellars. The juice undergoes alcoholic fermentation, the first step in a long process ending with ageing in wooden casks.

As a rule, all the wines undergo **"estufagem"** "stewing", a traditional practice in making Madeira wine, which consists of heating the liquid and keeping it at a constant temperature (50° Celsius). At an intermediate stage, the wines are stored in closed, airtight vessels for a minimum of 90 days. Some special reserves, particularly certain dated vintages, do not undergo this process but are matured more slowly in small capacity casks.

Modern wineries are a far cry from the more rudimentary processes used until around thirty years ago, that took longer to produce the end product.

Nowadays, reflecting market requirements and interna-

Pages 14-15:
Typical male costume carrying basket of fruit on shoulders; Borracheiro – wine must is transported from the press to the cellar in dried goatskin carriers; musicians from a folkloric group playing guitar and braguinha; typical peasant costume with cap.

tional quality standards, the Madeira Wine Institute exercises control over the quality of the wine and affixes a seal of quality to every bottle which allows the customer to confirm that it is genuine and declaring the alcohol content. The seal also certifies its origin and guarantees that the legislation applicable under international treaties has been complied with.

In the traditional wineries old wines of great quality can be found, whose value increases with age. They are guaranteed to delight all tastes and are suitable for any time of day. The grape varieties define their special characteristics, especially the times at which they should be served and enjoyed.

SERCIAL
SOLERA
1860

LEACOCK
MADEIRA

SELO DE GARANTIA
MADEIRA
815896
PORTUGAL

New Year's Eve at Funchal. The traditional firework display is one of the most famous tourist attractions of Madeira.

Funchal seen from Pico dos Barcelos.

MADEIRA

FUNCHAL

The city of Funchal was created on 21st August 1508 by royal charter of King Manuel I. It had been the first parish established on the island, in 1430, five years after it was first settled. It received its town charter in 1452, during the reign of King Afonso V, in recognition of its rapid development and expansion.

The port of Funchal began to be visited by Portuguese, Italian and Flemish sailors setting out on overseas voyages of exploration, and traders from Europe bringing new cultures, and customs and turning Funchal into an important trading entrepôt in the Atlantic.

The name Funchal derives from the sweet-smelling wild herb *Foeniculum vulgare*, commonly known as fennel (*funcho* in Portuguese), which was found growing profusely in the wild when the island was first settled.

The city is surrounded by mountainous slopes covered in vegetation. The backdrop of the mountains forms an enchanting natural amphitheatre, especially when viewed from the sea - a view about which books have raved over the years, ranking it at the head of the most beautiful landscapes described by writers in recent centuries.

Funchal is the largest municipality in the region. It contains ten parishes: Imaculado Coração de Maria, Santa Maria Maior, Monte, Santo António, São Roque, São Martinho, São Pedro, Sé, Santa Luzia and São Gonçalo.

Today's visitors will find Funchal a well-planned, modern and safe city, the equal of the most cosmopolitan in Europe, with interesting parks and public gardens, and rich in endemic plants and species. Its people are cordial and friendly, and welcome tourists. The warmth of the Funchalenses is well-known throughout the world. The city relies heavily on tourism and trade and understands how to treat its visitors well.

Funchal has a number of pedestrian-only streets, allowing visitors to walk around freely, and many es-

View of the harbour and bay of Funchal.

Monte cable car.

planades. It is a growing city with environmental and landscape protection policies set by the municipal authorities to prevent building in areas of outstanding natural beauty.

THE CATHEDRAL

The **Sé Catedral do Funchal** (*Cathedral Church of Funchal*) is a very fine piece of architecture. It was built on the orders of King Manuel I of Portugal who, while he was still Duke, issued orders in 1485 for the purchase of the site. It was built at the end of the 15th century under the supervision of Master Pêro Annes. It boasts one of the most beautiful ceilings of all Portuguese cathedrals, made from Madeira woods. Its interior decoration, like much else of its interior, reflects the Spanish-Arab and Romano-Gothic styles prevalent at the time.

The Bishop's Throne in the chancel is in the Flemish style, the main door has Gothic lines and the gilded carvings in the interior reveal characteristics of the exuberant Manueline period.

The Cathedral dates from a period of great prosperity in Madeira which encouraged the Portuguese colonists to plan and construct new buildings.

The building was consecrated in 1508. The seat of the parish, which had been at the Church of Nossa Senhora do Calhau, was transferred to the Cathedral, where it still remains, and the parish renamed **Paróquia da Sé** (*Cathedral Parish*). The church was not elevated to cathedral status until 12nd June 1514, following the creation of the diocese by papal bull of Pope Leo X. It was consecrated on 18th October 1517 by Bishop Duarte.

On 31st January 1533, Pope Clement VII, at the request of King João, elevated the Diocese of Funchal to the status of an Archdiocese, transferring spiritual jurisdiction over the island of Madeira from Tomar. With this change, the Diocese covered not merely the islands of the archipelago but also all the territories discovered or still to be discovered by the Portuguese. Its jurisdiction extended, therefore, over the whole of West and East Africa, Brazil and Asia. In 1539, the elevation to an Archdiocese was reconfirmed by Pope Paul III. Its first and only Archbishop, with the style of Primate, was Dom Martinho de Portugal.

Subsequently, the Dioceses of Goa, Angra, Cape Verde, São Tomé and São Salvador da Bahía, in Brazil, were separated from Funchal. In 1550, it ceased to be a Metropolitan See and fell under the jurisdiction of the Archbishopric of Lisbon.

The Cathedral (15th century) seen from the side of the Sacristy. The courtyard contains a century-old palm tree.

Nave of Igreja da Sé.

Ceiling of the Cathedral chancel lined with Madeiran woods.

The first black bishop of modern times was Dom Henrique, son of the King of the Congo, who exercised his ministry here as Vicar-General of the Diocese of Funchal.

The Cathedral dominates the Largo da Sé, where Avenida Arriaga begins, one of Funchal's principal roads and the artery for traffic heading for the parishes of the municipality of Funchal.

MUSEU DE ARTE SACRA
(MUSEUM OF RELIGIOUS ART)

Museu de Arte Sacra do Funchal (*Funchal Museum of Religious Art*) was founded in 1955. It is housed in the former **Paço Episcopal** (*Bishop's Palace*), commissioned in 1594 and laid out by the royal master-builder Jerónimo Jorge in 1604, on the orders of the seventh Bishop of Funchal, Dom Luís Figueiredo de Lemos. This complex of buildings, lying between Rua do Bispo and Praça do Município (or Largo do Colégio) was planned as the seat of the diocese and a seminary. It was destroyed by an earthquake in 1748 but was rebuilt two years later.

The building has been added to extensively over the years. Over one of the doors, there is an inscription with the date 1750, the year of the last major works to the building.

The **Museu Diocesano de Arte Sacra** (*Diocesan Museum of Religious Art*) contains valuable artistic collections that are well worth visiting. The collections were formed from objects selected over the years from various churches and chapels in the Diocese of Funchal, many of them now disused. Of particular note is an excellent collection of Flemish paintings from the 16th to 18th centuries.

The collections in the **Museu de Arte Sacra do Funchal** have recently been reclassified and the exhibitions re-arranged to offer new perspectives. Scholars can now carry out research on the displayed works, many of them by unusual northern European artists and some still unattributed.

A large number of the Flemish paintings that have come down to us were bought by Madeirans from Flemish traders who took on cargoes of sugar in Madeira. The works were commissioned from the great Masters and painted in their studios in Bruges and Antwerp. The representation of Flemish art in the archipelago is remarkable. The work of the famous Flemish school (painting, sculpture and gold and silver work) can be seen in several places, most especially in the **Museu de Arte Sacra**. Here can be seen panels painted by the leading artists of the time, triptychs or altarpieces combining painting and sculpture, as well as other works of visual art. Amongst the signatures on the most prominent works in the **Museu de Arte Sacra** are those of Gerard David, Van Cleve, Provost, Pieter Coecke, Van Aelst, Jan Gossart de Mabuse and Marinus van Reymerswaele. Flemish art, which signals a golden period of prosperity in Portugal since the works were acquired from the proceeds of rising exports, can also be seen in several parish churches in Madeira. Visitors particularly interested in Flemish art should visit the parish churches of Ribeira Brava, Ponta do Sol, Caniçal and Porto Santo.

The Museum also houses a large collection of sculptures, gold and silver altar plate, liturgical vestments and Portuguese paintings of the 15th to 18th centuries.

Part of the so-called **"Tesouro da Sé"** (*Cathedral Treasure*) is housed in the **Museu de Arte Sacra**. Of particular note are the gold Processional Cross given by King Manuel I and many objects in silver, a metal much used in the 16th and 17th centuries as the huge traffic of the "silver galleons" from Castile gave encouragement to its use.

Facing page:
Top, Museum of Religious Art (18th century) seen from Praça do Município; bottom, Portuguese silverware urn (18th century) and Processional Cross in gold donated by King Manuel I (1514).

This page:
Top, Flemish painting from a group of works by an anonymous painter working in Bruges in the first quarter of the 16th century; bottom, Flemish sculptures in polychrome oak (16th century).

Funchal Town Hall (18ᵗʰ century).

MUNICÍPIO DO FUNCHAL
(*MUNICIPALITY OF FUNCHAL*)

As far back as the time of Prince Henry the Navigator, when cereals and subsistence crops were still its mainstay, Funchal received its first charter, around 1452 to 1454, elevating it to the status of a town and capital of the municipality. During the second half of the 15ᵗʰ century, the cultivation of sugar cane developed strongly, with sugar cane fields spreading all over the south coast of the island from Machico to Fajã da Ovelha. Funchal, because of its location, profited most from this boom in sugar production. In the closing years of the 15ᵗʰ century, and with Manuel, Duke of Beja now heading the Order of Christ, he set about planning and redeveloping this go-ahead, prosperous town and ordered the construction of the **Paços do Concelho** (*Town Hall*) and the Tabeliães (*Notary's Office*), completed in 1491. At the start of the 16ᵗʰ century, in 1508, Funchal was elevated to city status, and a few years later, in 1514, it was made the seat of a diocese. Still later, following the creation of the dioceses of Angra, Cape Verde, S. Tomé and Goa, it became the seat of an archdiocese, with these new bishoprics becoming suffragan dioceses. At that time, the city extended along a long riverside road, known by various names at different times in its history, such as Santa Maria, dos Caixeiros, Alfândega and dos Mercadores. Side streets grew up at right angles to it, bordering the three streams that cross the wide valley, and leading into the mountains. The earliest and principal of these was Rua Direita, starting at the mouth of the João Gomes and Santa Luzia streams. The vine was introduced by the first settlers with the encouragement of Prince Henry the Navigator. As early as 1455, the Venetian navigator Luís de Cadamosto, visiting Madeira, commented on the excellence of Madeira wines, particularly the **malvasias** (*malmseys*) from

the island of Creta, and their export. By the mid-17ᵗʰ century, the famous English playwright, William Shakespeare, was alluding to the fame and the importance of exports of Madeiran malmsey by arranging for the Duke of Clarence, brother of King Edward IV of England, to choose death by drowning in a butt of this wine. During the course of the 19ᵗʰ century, the island of Madeira and Funchal became a European romantic legend, with the visits to the island of the Empress Sissi of Austria, Queen Adelaide of England, the Dowager Empress of Brazil and her daughter Princess Maria Amélia, the future Emperor of Mexico and his wife, Princess Charlotte of Belgium and many other famous members of European noble families. The island and the gentle hillsides of Funchal gained fame as a spa resort and the city became almost an indispensable part of the early international tourism of the Grand Tour. From the closing years of the 18ᵗʰ century, the city spread out along the coast as far as Monte, with the growth of small manor houses set in private parks with exotic trees, belvederes overlooking the roads and summerhouses, giving birth to the traditional Madeiran "quinta", while many of the townhouses became commercial establishments.

Marble statue "Leda and the Swan" (1941) in the interior courtyard of Funchal Town Hall.

Statue in the Municipal Garden pond.

Bust of Simon Bolivar in the Municipal Garden.

IGREJA DO COLÉGIO

Construction of the Igreja do Colégio, or Church of **São João Evangelista** (*St. John the Evangelist*), began in 1624 and was completed around 1647. It is a church of Jesuit foundation, with a long, high nave and a wide chancel, as will be readily noticed. The nave is lined with identical side chapels dedicated to various saints. The church forms part of the Jesuit College complex, the main building of which is occupied by the University of Madeira. The church's dedication to St. John the Evangelist reflects the fact that lessons at the College began on 6 May 1570, the date on which the saint's martyrdom in Rome is celebrated.

The church's furnishings include a group of gilded carved altarpieces dated 1647, 1648, 1654 and 1660, and a number of 17th and 18th century statues. The frescos on the ceiling and the decorated roof tiles date from the 17th and 18th centuries.

The interior of the church, like the **Sé Catedral do Funchal** (*Cathedral of Funchal*), contains objects of great value. The high altar is regarded as a masterpiece of Madeiran carving of the period, created by the finest artists in the Kingdom. Many of the altarpieces were painted specially for the church by famous artists of the time, both Portuguese and Flemish.

Facade of Igreja do Colégio (17th century) or São João Evangelista.

Nave of Igreja do Colégio.

Main entrance of the Dr. Frederico de Freitas House Museum (18th century).

Winter Garden and sitting room with 18th century furniture.

DR. FREDERICO DE FREITAS ETHNOGRAPHIC MUSEUM

The Dr. Frederico de Freitas Ethnographic Museum is an 18th century building situated near the Church of São Pedro.

In earlier times the home of the collector and jurist Dr. Frederico Augusto de Cunha Freitas, who bequeathed his valuable collection of furniture and furnishings to the region, the museum opened to the public in 1988 and displays a remarkable collection of artefacts tracing the artistic and cultural developments of recent centuries.

Metal objects from China and North Africa, 17th and 18th century wood carvings, a collection of jugs, milk jugs and jars numbering approximately 2000 pieces, ceramics, religious sculptures, furniture, and Persian, Moorish-Spanish, Dutch and Portuguese prints and tiles (from the 13th to the 19th century) are just a few examples of the fabulous variety of pieces that can be seen in the museum.

In addition to its permanent collection, the museum also houses temporary exhibitions on related themes.

QUINTA DAS CRUZES MUSEUM

Quinta das Cruzes Museum is the most visited museum in Funchal. It is a listed property including a 16th century dwelling house once lived in by the first Lords Captain and their successors, a chapel dedicated to **Nossa Senhora da Piedade** (*Our Lady of Mercy*) completed in 1692, a park with an orchid house, anthuriums and several species of trees, directly linked to the Madeira Botanical Gardens, and an archaeological park housing a variety of artefacts such as stone escutcheons and tombstones, Manueline windows, gargoyles, etc.

Its name derives from the Festival of the Crosses, traditionally associated with the Minho region in mainland Portugal. The first building was erected in the 15th century, but a new house was constructed on the same site in the following century which was altered and added to over the years, making it a mixture of styles from different architectural periods through to the 19th century. Nuno Martiniano de Freitas was the last heir to live in the Quinta, after the law of 11st May 1863 extinguished the practice of leaving properties to the

eldest son and required estates to be divided between all the successors.

The museum's contents include a number of collections of historical, artistic or cultural importance which have been added to as new artefacts were acquired. The original collections were donated by César Filipe Gomes and include furniture, faience ware, paintings, terracotta Nativity scenes, chinaware, glass objects and other artefacts of ethnographic interest.

The work of Portuguese gold and silversmiths is also featured, as part of a collection of plate donated by João Wetzler, another collector who contributed to the enhancement of the museum's collections.

Main facade of Quinta das Cruzes Museum (16th century).

Gilded silver salver.

Pot with lid of the East India Company (late 18th century).

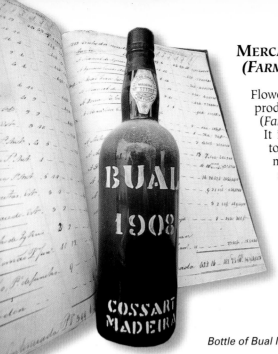

MERCADO DOS LAVRADORES
(FARMERS' MARKET)

Flowers, fruit, vegetables and many varieties of fresh fish are amongst the products that can be found on sale at the **Mercado dos Lavradores** (*Farmers' Market*), brought from all over the island.

It is a colourful and lively scene, bustling with stallholders and customers who come here to do their shopping. The market is one of the most popular attractions for visitors to Madeira for its unique and seemingly endless display of the wide variety of fruit and vegetables grown on the island.

The bustling stallholders who sell the produce make a fascinating sight because they keep alive the traditions and day-to-day vitality of the Mercado dos Lavradores. The market is at its busiest at the end of the week, on Fridays and Saturdays, when the produce is sold direct from the growers.

The market also has a flower section, yet another attractive display of colour. Cut flowers can be bought here at farm gate prices to take back home.

Bottle of Bual Madeira Wine.

"Fish Market"

In the **Praça do Peixe** (*Fish Hall*), the fish are laid out on granite slabs. In addition to scabbard-fish and tuna, the traditional island species, we can find many varieties of fish and shellfish caught by local boats in the teeming seas off Madeira and the Azores.

Kerb layers in Funchal old town.

Members of the Camacha Folkloric Group
in the Funchal Flower Procession.

Playing cards in a Funchal park.

THE STATUE OF ZARCO

The wide, two-lane Avenida Arriaga, offers pedestrians a wonderful, tree-shaded area for a stroll. The avenue traverses the city from the Sé Cathedral to the Prince Henry Rotonda which leads into Avenida do Infante, via the Gardens and the Municipal Theater.
Just opposite the Bank of Portugal is the statue of João Gonçalves Zarco.
The Portuguese navigator, who began colonizing the island faces south and seems to be extending a welcome to all those arriving at the port of Funchal. The statue was

made by Francisco Franco, a sculptor from Madrid who had studied in Portugal.

Avenida Arriaga, Funchal.

Entrance of the Bank of Portugal and a statue of João Gonçalves Zarco, Madeira's discoverer, in the foreground.

Flower and fruit sellers in the streets of Funchal.

Funchal is home to a wonderful collection of display tiles, the creation of which has been an art in Portugal since the seventeenth century. The most noteworthy examples are exhibited in the Dr. Frederico Freitas Museum Centre. Around a century ago, it was also common to decorate houses occupied by noble families and other outstanding social figures with panels of display tiles, designed by prestigious national artists. At the entrance to the Regional Government Palace, in Avenida Zarco, there are walls filled with tiles that were specially created to decorate the main building entrance, opening out onto the marble staircases leading to the chamber known as 'Salão Nobre'.

Views of the main facade of São Lourenço Palace (16th century) from Avenida do Mar.

PALÁCIO DE SÃO LOURENÇO

The Palácio de São Lourenço is a historical monument which includes the **Fortaleza** (*Fortress*), begun in the first half of the 16th century and completed in the reign of King Felipe I. The Palácio proper contains the state reception rooms dating from the last quarter of the 18th century and courtyard gardens. It dominates the bay of Funchal and the port, and was one of the first major buildings in the city.

It was the official residence of the Lords Captain of Funchal up to the time of King Felipe I and the headquarters of the Spanish garrison on the island until 1640. It then became the residence of the Military Governors-General, a title that persisted until the establishment of constitutional government in 1834, after which the Madeira archipelago was ruled by civil governors. In 1836, the Fortaleza-Palácio complex was divided into a military part, to the east (now occupied by the Madeira Military Area Command) and the Palácio, the official residence of the Civil Governor.

Following the establishment of autonomous regional government in 1976, the part formerly occupied by the Civil Governor became the official residence of the Minister of the Republic for the Autonomous Region of Madeira.

The construction of the Fortaleza-Palácio de São Lourenço in the 16th century and its history are inextricably intertwined with the history of Madeira itself and its key events.

Funchal Marina.

Mermaid Sculpture in Funchal Marina.

View of Funchal at dusk from the quay.

MARINA

Funchal Marina was built next to the city's former quay to provide anchorage for the small pleasure craft and yachts that began to call at the port with greater frequency after the 1970s. Because of its location, Madeira is a port of call between two continents and many small craft sailing from Europe to America call here.

Funchal Marina is now a major tourist and leisure attraction. Restaurants and bars have sprung up in its pleasant surroundings by the edge of the sea which are popular with residents and tourists alike. Ashore, there is a range of specialist facilities for sailors calling at the island. The city's official and public bodies are able to meet the basic needs of the sailors of many nationalities who choose Funchal as a place to relax for a few days before picking up the trade winds that will take them safely to South America or the marvellous islands of the Caribbean, the destinations of most of the yachts that call at Madeira.

Funchal Marina is also the home port of many of the boats used for tourist cruises along the coast and for big game fishing, a sport that attracts many visitors to Madeira from North America, Great Britain and France.

Santa Catarina Park with Ponta do Garajau in the background, and Chapel of Santa Catarina; bottom, statue of Christopher Colombus in Santa Catarina Park, and monument and statue to Prince Henry (1394-1460) by Leopoldo de Almeida (1947).

PARQUE DE SANTA CATARINA

The Parque de Santa Catarina, also known as the Parque da Cidade, is a large landscaped park overlooking the port of Funchal.

Apart from its rich planting, with a wide variety of trees and bedding plants, excellently maintained by the municipal gardeners, the Parque de Santa Catarina contains three monuments that recall the history of Madeira, associated as they are with the time of the Voyages of Discovery.

The first is the chapel of Santa Catarina, over four hundred years old, where Mass was said for the first time in Madeira. It was built by the first Portuguese sailors to reach the island.

Another important monument is the Statue of Prince Henry the Navigator. It was erected by the People of Madeira in honour of the founder of the **Escola Náutica de Sagres** (*Nautical School at Sagres*), in the south of Portugal, where the first navigators were trained, and the man who was the driving force behind the Voyages of Discovery.

The other statue is of Christopher Columbus. This is of more recent date but it completes the circle, since it honours the man who discovered the New World. Columbus lived in Madeira and he married the daughter of a Portuguese dignitary here.

The Parque de Santa Catarina is very popular with both locals and visitors. It has a terrace with a café, a variety of tropical birds and a lagoon. Its trees provide much welcomed shade.

CASINO DA MADEIRA
MUNICIPAL SWIMMING POOL

On the outskirts of Funchal, towards Câmara de Lobos, is an area known to residents and many tourists as the hotel strip. It is one of the best spots on the island, not just for its pleasant climate but also because it has the longest hours of sunshine throughout the year.

The hotel strip, from Funchal to Ponta da Cruz, with the amphitheatre of vineyards at Estreito de Câmara de Lobos as its backdrop, is home to the most important hotels in Madeira's capital. It also houses spa complexes, restaurants and bars linked by a coastal promenade extending between the two major tourist attractions of the Lido swimming pools and the bay of Praia Formosa.

Here also are the Madeira Casino, open every weekday until three in the morning, and the Hotel Carlton, whose opening in 1972 marked an important period of reorganisation of the island's hotel industry, with the arrival of the international hotel chains. Today, the area between the Casino and the Lido is the first choice for visitors to Madeira. The majority of tourist accommodation on the island is located here.

Madeira Casino designed by architect Óscar Niemeyer and Carlton Hotel swimming pools and solarium.

Lido municipal swimming pool and Cavacas dock in Ponta da Cruz.

EMPRESS SISSI IN MADEIRA

Although Empress Sissi's trips and stays in Madeira are well documented and confirmed, there is a certain amount of mystery surrounding them, and nowadays these provide a strong attraction for Austrian tourists coming to Madeira. Empress Elisabeth Amalie (Sissi) was considered to be the most beautiful monarch in the world. She measured 1.72 m in height, never weighed more than 50 kilos and maintained a waistline of 50 cm. As well as her starvation diets, she had a gymnastics room installed in the palace, and was also considered to be the best horse-rider in Europe.

In 1859, when Empress Sissi of Austria decided to leave her husband and children, she took refuge in Possenhofen (Germany) and started to make longer and longer journeys, living as a semi-recluse in Madeira, where she treated herself for the beginnings of tuberculosis. The island had the right characteristics, thanks to its mild climate, and was sought after by many members of the European royalty and other rich families.

Infante Dom Luís, representing the Portuguese Royal Family, came to Madeira in 1861, to be present at the departure of Empress Sissi from the island. The empress had stayed in Quinta Vigia, as before, on which site there is now a hotel and casino.

The local authorities had reserved one of the wings of the São Lourenço Palace for Sissi, prepared the year before on the King's orders, but the empress always preferred to stay in Quinta Vigia, a house with large verandas and ample gardens with a view to the sea.

EMPEROR CHARLES I OF AUSTRIA IN MADEIRA

The former emperor of Austria, Charles of Hapsburg, arrived in Madeira on the morning of 19th November 1921, aboard the English cruiser Cardiff, and proceeded to disembark at the jetty of Pontinha, in Funchal, accompanied by his wife, the former Empress Zita. He travelled to Vila Vitória, in front of what is now the Casino, and set up residence there.

The former emperor Charles had renounced his leadership of the new State, and had withdrawn from the armistice with the allies in 1921, after the separation of Austria and Hungary, which both declared themselves republics.

In 1918 the Austro-Hungarian forces had been defeated on all fronts; the nationalist groups within the Empire organised national councils that functioned as autonomous governments. The Slavs in the south met together in Zagreb in October 1918, and proposed a union with Serbia, while the Czechs declared an independent republic.

In January 1922 the former Empress left the island to fetch her children, who where studying in Switzerland, and returned on 2nd February, together with the princes Francis Otto, Adelaide Mary, Robert Charles and Charles Luis. The whole family began to live in the parish of Monte, on the farm of banker Luis da Rocha Machado, from the 18th of the same month.

The former emperor Charles passed away on 1st April

1922, and his body was interred at the Monte parish church on the 5th of that month, whereupon the Empress decided to leave the island.

BOTANICAL GARDENS

Madeira Botanical Gardens, situated on the outskirts of Funchal, were established in 1960, when the Quinta do Bom Sucesso was bought from the Reid family, who built the earliest hotel still operating on the island, Reid's Palace.

The Botanical Gardens are situated three kilometres from the city centre in a superb setting, at the mid-point of the Funchal natural amphitheatre, with wide views over the bay and the port. The Gardens lie on the south slope of a valley at altitudes between 200 and 350 metres, providing a range of conditions suitable for growing a lush variety of plants. The whole property, with a planted area of over 35,000 square metres, is a picture of harmonious forms and contrasting colours. The planted areas contain over 2000 exotic plants from every continent, including orchids, bird-of-paradise flowers, anthuriums, magnolias, azaleas, bromeliads, cacti, palms, ferns and many other species, growing side by side and as well-adapted as in their original habitats.

Cycads, palm trees and Laurisilva are among the more than 2,500 botanical species on display in this garden.

It is this diversity of plants, allied with the most beautiful of the island's flowers, that gives the Gardens their singular beauty.

Ever since their foundation, the regional government has invested heavily in the Botanical Gardens, turning them into a veritable centre of science and learning, where both Portuguese and foreign university students and researchers can extend their knowledge and conduct research, and school students can begin to explore the fascinating world of botany.

Several Madeiran plants threatened with extinction are currently being studied, and in the planted areas, it is possible to observe the propagation of plants thought to be extinct or under threat.

The Botanical Gardens perform a vital role in the understanding and conservation of the Madeiran flora by maintaining living collections of plants available for study for sci-

entific research purposes, conservation and environmental education. Next door to the Botanical Gardens there is a reserve for tropical birds, which live happily alongside the many species of small birds that flit from tree to tree and are yet another treasure of this Nature Park.

The buildings of the Botanical Gardens house a Museum of Natural History and a Herbarium, which are open every day from 9 a.m. to 6 p.m. Visitors can join guided tours conducted by specialists.

Macaws, cockatoos and other exotic birds in Loiro Park next to the Botanical Garden.

41

Golf

Golf has come to acquire considerable prominence in recent years, in Madeira as elsewhere. It is a very important market segment in the promotion of a holiday destination and in developing its tourist potential.

Madeira has two golf courses, both only a few minutes from the main hotels in Funchal and the Caniço area, where the island's best hotels are situated.

Both courses lie in a plateau setting amidst luxuriant vegetation, and boast astounding views.

The Santo da Serra Golf Course (half an hour from Funchal) has 27 holes and is the most important in Madeira. Every spring, the Madeira Open, a tournament forming part of the P.G.A. European Tour, is held here. Some of the most famous names in the world of golf have played here. It was designed by Robert Trent Jones.

Palheiro Golf Course is situated in the mountains overlooking Funchal, and enjoys fantastic views over the bay and the city. It has 18 holes and was designed in 1993 by Cabell Robinson. It lies within the park of the Quinta do Palheiro Ferreiro, a property with extensive gardens, exotic trees and a wide variety of birds. A survey has identified 291 species, but only about 40 of these are resident in abundance at the Quinta.

Santo da Serra Golf Course.

according to the publication "Elucidário Madeirense". It was where the people came together in the early days of colonisation, gathered around the site of a small worshipping point, dedicated to Nossa Senhora da Incarnação, later named Nossa Senhora do Monte (*Our Lady of the Mountain*) due to the relief of the land.

The parish is spread out amongst leafy orchards and farm estates belonging to old noblemen. Monte was the first inland parish in the city of Funchal. At only a few kilometres from the best-known port in Madeira, it is situated at a sideways angle, amply exposed by the wonderful amphitheatre of the city. In the nineteenth century, Monte was sought after by many noble families in Madeira, who built their holiday homes here. Later, it also became the destination chosen by many foreigners, mainly British and German visitors who came to settle on the island, as well as merchants who passed through with trading boats to the West Indies and Africa, and considered Monte the perfect site for a few weeks rest, and to adapt to the climate of those lands. The first hotels

MONTE

The parish of Monte is one of the most picturesque areas of Funchal. It grew from a parish created from a populated settlement belonging to the first man to have been born in Madeira, the son of Gonçalo Aires Ferreira, "the most distinguished companion of Gonçalves Zarco in the discovery of the archipelago",

on the island were built in Monte, in tree-lined estates, using typically Northern European construction models. There are many beautiful gardens in Monte, and on 15th August it hosts the Festival to the Patron Saint of Madeira, Nossa Senhora do Monte, in which many natives of Madeira, even those working abroad, come together in this parish to celebrate, and particularly to return their promises to the saint.

Carreiros (*Basket carriages*)

The typical "Monte basket carriages" begin their descent at the bottom of the steps of the majestic and emblematic Igreja de Nossa Senhora do Monte.

Made of a wicker chair with upholstered seat and back, they can take two or three passengers and are commonly used by tourists after a visit to the picturesque parish of Monte.

Underneath the wicker chair there are two wooden sticks like skis which enable it to slide down the pathways, controlled by ropes held in the strong, capable hands and arms of two "carreiros", who stand for most of the trip on a wooden platform behind the wicker chair.

The basket carriages can either end their journey halfway down at Livramento or continue to Funchal. An exhilarating experience, with the lack of protection from the front bringing a rush of adrenaline as passengers' faces defy the wind and the speed of the descent. It is also a stunning ex-

perience, giving passengers an unforgettable view over Funchal Bay.

Facade of Igreja do Monte (1747) dedicated to Nossa Senhora do Monte, patron saint of Madeira.

Interior of Igreja do Monte.

Capela do Largo da Fonte in Monte and Tomb of Emperor Charles of Austria inside Igreja do Monte.

Image of Nossa Senhora do Monte, much worshipped by the people of Madeira.

IGREJA DO MONTE

The church Igreja do Monte is the most visited religious monument in Madeira. Set on one of Funchal's slopes, its white walls make it visible by day and continuous illumination make it stand out by night. Thousands of people, both pilgrims and tourists, travel there throughout the year, and Nossa Senhora do Monte is also the Island's Patron Saint.

The parish was established by the Diocesan Bishop on 9th February 1565 and named Nossa Senhora do Monte. The primitive Hermitage dedicated to Nossa Senhora da Incarnação came into being in 1470.

The old hermitage was demolished in 1741 to build the new church dedicated to Nossa Senhora do Monte and consecrated in 1747. One year after the new temple was built, on the night of 31st March to 1st April 1748, it was destroyed by a violent earthquake that left only the side walls standing. The current-day church contains a main chapel with an image of Nossa Senhora do Monte, worshipped by the people of Madeira, the Capela do (*chapel of*) Santíssimo Sacramento and a tomb containing the remains of Emperor Charles of Austria, who took refuge in Madeira.

The festival of Nossa Senhora do Monte is held on 15th August, bringing thousands of believers, many from abroad, mainly emigrants.

CÂMARA DE LOBOS

The parish of Câmara de Lobos, founded around 1430, is one of the oldest in Madeira. The mother church of the parish was originally the chapel of **Espírito Santo** (*The Holy Spirit*), founded by João Gonçalves Zarco, but was later transferred to the church of São Sebastião.

It was this traditional fishing village, five kilometres from Funchal, that Sir Winston Churchill was inspired to paint in the early 1950s when he visited the island. The famous photograph showing the elderly statesman, with his ubiquitous cigar, sitting at his easel under a sunshade painting the fishing boats that are a feature of the bay, has become indelibly associated with the name of Câmara de Lobos.

The name **Câmara de Lobos** (*The Seals' Debating Chamber*) was given to it by João Gonçalves Zarco and Tristão Vaz Teixeira because of the shape of the bay (debating chamber) and the fact that there were many seals in the area. Initially, the islet was completely encircled by water but an earthquake brought down part of the Pico da Torre and the resulting landslip filled the site where today's town centre stands.

In addition to its charming bay, Câmara de Lobos contains a number of places of interest, such as the Pico da Torre, with its views over the town and the port, especially attractive at night. The viewpoint is situated on the road to Estreito de Câmara de Lobos. The Pico da Torre is soon spotted on the right, affording views of the bay and town of Câmara de Lobos, and the parishes of São Martinho, Estreito de Câmara de Lobos, Campanário and Cabo Girão.

Câmara de Lobos is the home of "Poncha", a mixture of lemon juice, honey and sugar-cane spirit, readily available in the many traditional local bars. If you enjoy taking photographs, you will adore the landscapes of Câmara de Lobos and its inhabitants.

View of Câmara de Lobos and fishing harbour.

Restaurant evoking the visit of former British statesman Winston Churchill to Câmara de Lobos in the early fifties.

Drying dogfish, known as Câmara de Lobos cod.

The fajãs *(farming land) at Cabo Girão are only accessible by boat or along dangerous paths.*

CABO GIRÃO

For the visitor, exploring Madeira means making many circuits of the island. The route between Funchal and Porto Moniz passes Cabo Girão, a must on anybody's itinerary.

No visitor can fail to be impressed by the height and steepness of the precipice. This first dramatic impression makes it easy to overlook the toil and sweat of the early colonists who carved terraces out of the cliff face to plant their crops, and created roads and tunnels. What most hits us as we take a second look, though, is the Herculean strength of those who managed to transform the vertiginous cliff face into cornfields, vineyards and cane fields.

This effort is plain to see at Cabo Girão and all around. But the most breathtaking thing is its height above the sea. It lies half way between Estreito de Câmara de Lobos and Quinta Grande at an altitude of 580 metres, and is the highest promontory in Europe and the second highest in the world. The Cape affords a vast and stunning panorama from Estreito de Câmara de Lobos to the bay of Funchal, with spectacular views over the sea and the beaches.

Visitors are particularly recommended to look for the farm plots "**fajãs**" perched on terraces below the viewpoint.

CURRAL DAS FREIRAS

On the way to Curral das Freiras, a turning to the right leads to the viewpoint of Eira do Serrado. From here on a clear day, one can see the parish of Curral das Freiras nestling in the bottom of the valley, inside what is thought to be the crater of one of the many volcanoes that, millions of years ago, gave birth to the island of Madeira. This version is supported by some studies, while others, in the absence of definitive scientific evidence, claim that the appearance of the crater is due simply to erosion. Whatever the truth of the matter, it bears a close resemblance to certain landscapes in the Canary Islands, of all which are also of volcanic origin.

The viewpoint of Eira do Serrado lies at an altitude of 1095 metres. From here, visitors can enjoy spectacularly beautiful views, not only of the parish of Curral das Freiras, but also of the surrounding mountains.

The parish of Curral das Freiras is one of the most picturesque on the island. It acquired its name (*Nuns' Farmyard*) in 1560, when it became the refuge for the nuns of the Convent of Santa Clara in Funchal fleeing from French Lutheran pirates, and who found this an ideal hiding place since it is one of the few places in Madeira that is not visible from the sea and, in addition, is very hard to reach. The return journey to Funchal is via the sole road to Curral das Freiras. The village has restaurants and bars and a church which is worth visiting.

The parish of Curral das Freiras has benefited from several public works projects. Improved roads to the more inaccessible places has encouraged people to remain in the parish, whereas before they tended to work away from home and only return at weekends. Agriculture has also developed as it is now easier to get produce to market.

Curral das Freiras inside the crater of an old volcano.

Interior of Curral das Freiras parish church

Pastelaria *(café/cake shop) in the centre of Curral das Freiras.*

The town of Ribeira Brava; left, Parish Church; bottom, São Bento Fort at the town's entrance.

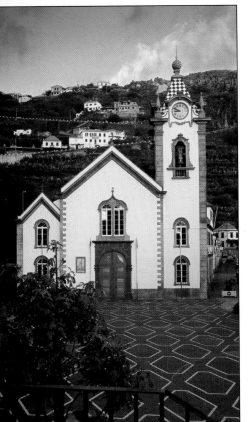

RIBEIRA BRAVA

Ribeira Brava is situated on Madeira's south-west coast. Although around thirty kilometres from the easiest access points to Funchal, thanks to the express way it is a centre for traffic distribution to the West and North of the island.

It boasts several cafés and esplanades and is a pleasing place to spend a few hours enjoying the landscape. There are also a few hotels and it is one of the places outside the traditional urbanisation areas of Funchal where construction of residential apartments has developed fastest.

Ribeira Brava was one of the island's first parishes and has been inhabited since the early days.

Founded in 1440, it was named by João Gonçalves Zarco, who found a river with wild waters descending towards the sea. In the hard winters this frequently arrives at the river mouth at a furious rate.

The source of the river lies at an altitude of 327 metres and it flows for 8 kilometres, the road to Encumeada running alongside, providing an excellent starting point for breathtaking walks.

Also in the municipality of Ribeira Brava are the parishes of Ribeira Brava, Campanário, Tabua and Serra de Água.

52

PONTA DO SOL

The name Ponta do Sol (*Point of the Sun*) owes its name to a sharp and pointed rock which enters the sea and reflects the sun's rays.

It was first settled in 1425 and achieved the status of town in 1501.

Considered the island's warmest municipality with the most hours of sunshine, Ponta do Sol is made up of the parishes of Madalena do Mar, Canhas and Ponta do Sol. Its fertile soil has been used since the beginning for the so-called rich crops, and at the time of colonisation it was one of the most active centres for agricultural production, especially sugar cane.

The town of Ponta do Sol is located by the sea and has a pebble beach which is very popular with the people of Madeira. Near the beach, a four-star hotel along with other small but high quality units have given it a new direction.

Madalena do Mar is well-known as a typical fishing area and for the pretty coast road connecting the two ends, where the calm water beach is also an attraction. A hotel resort is also planned for the area so as to take full advantage of its favourable characteristics for Tourism.

Ponta do Sol Parish Church.

Ponta do Sol bay.

ENCUMEADA

High summits are common to the relief geography of the island of Madeira, and the name Encumeada describes the high mountains from which great panoramic views are possible, where vast, distant horizons stretch out before the viewer.

The Encumeada de São Vicente is one of the most renowned regions on the island, located between the parishes of Serra d'Água and São Vicente on the northern coast. It is halfway between the two parishes, and is the highest point reached by the regional road as it winds between them. It is located at an altitude of above one thousand metres, on one of the most characteristic mountains in a range stretching across the centre of the island.

From this lookout point, visitors enjoy an extraordinarily wide-ranging view, especially on clear and bright days where one can sea two coasts of the island; in the South towards Ribeira Brava, and to the North, towards São Vicente. At the Encumeada lookout point you can spend a few pensive moments and feel really at the centre of the island. Here, you really get the feeling that the island is just a patch of land surrounded by sea, even if the Western and Eastern coastlines are not quite visible.

In Encumeada do not forget to try the famous "poncha". It is a mixture of sugar cane brandy with lemon juice and honey. The "poncha" served at the Bar at Encumeada is typical and worth tasting.

SERRA D'ÁGUA

The parish of Serra d'Água takes its name from an industrial infrastructure on the riverside, and is located in a wide, deep and closed valley, surrounded by high mountains.

It was here, in 1953, that the first Hydroelectric Plant on the island was built. The charge chamber of the

Hydroelectric Plant is fed by the Levada do Norte, after it passes through the tunnel to the south of the island, near Encumeada.

This was once a thoroughfare point, halfway up the mountain to Ribeira Brava in the south, or to São Vicente in the North, and has now been split in two by a new road connecting to the tunnel that passes through the magnificent mountain of Encumeada and which has reduced the distance between the North and South of the island by several kilometres. The new access route has also facilitated development in the parish, making transport easier and allowing access to areas that had previously only been reached by footpaths and tracks. Improved access has led to the construction of new houses, improving the value of the land.

Serra d'Água is an agricultural parish, and has resisted the process of desertification that some rural areas have experienced. Some families have begun settling here now that they have greater access and do not have to live close to their workplaces.

LOMBO DO MOURO

The lookout point 'Lombo do Mouro' on the road connecting Encumeada to Bica da Cana, in Paúl da Serra, offers one of the best views over the inland part of the island. Here, there is a small shelter built for the Forest Guard.

From the lookout point there is a wide view over the valley of the Serra d'Água river and the parish Ribeira Brava, which begins there, and stretches right to the sea. On clear days, the panorama is overwhelming. At the lookout point, travellers feel part of the giant picture, surrounded by high peaks, some sharp, made from dark basaltic rock, and others which are softer and sweeping down with verdant slopes, where water drops hundreds of metres to the river in a short space of time, feeding the hydro-electric plant in Serra d'Água.

A new road passes by Lombo do Mouro, which was built recently in the seventies across the face of Paúl da Serra towards the parish of Santa, in Portas da Vila, Porto Moniz. The Lombo do Mouro, site of harsh and wild winds, is one of the most hostile areas of the island, but also the site with one of the best panoramas. Its aggressive and imposing beauty reflects the great diversity to be found on the island of Madeira.

Facing page:
View of the rock formations at Encumeada towards Lombo do Mouro.

Top, Parish of Serra d'Água.

Left, Encumeada belvedere.

PAÚL DA SERRA

Paúl da Serra is a plateau located at 1400 metres in altitude. From the top of the plateau, the plain stretches towards Bica da Cana, where the old shepherds' shelter was turned into a hostel, near the road which leads to the mouth of Encumeada.

In order to reach Paúl da Serra, visitors can go via Porto Moniz, at the extreme Northwest of Madeira, or via Calheta. However, these are the longest and most difficult routes to follow. It is easier to enter Encumeada, practically at the centre of the island, following the old regional road halfway between the parishes of Ribeira Brava and São Vicente.

Paúl da Serra is a very cold region, with permanent fogs and high wind. There are several wind turbines installed here to produce electrical energy, a system which has proved extremely important to the regional production of electricity, given that in only a few years it has become responsible for five percent of the total energy output provided to the region's consumers. This is very reasonable in a region which does not have great water resources.

Bica da Cana is a grazing ground for several flocks of sheep and cattle. Drivers should be careful, as the fog can be heavy, and less-experienced drivers could be caught out by an unexpected animal blocking the road.

On a clear day, with a bright sky, it can be an extremely beautiful and calming place to walk. The landscape is a little different to that found in the lower areas of the island and the vegetation is dense and lush. There is also a Natural Reserve belonging to the Laurisilva Forest, and so it is advisable to obey the laws imposed by current legislation.

Herd of sheep at Bica da Cana.

Paúl da Serra plateau.

View of Madalena do Mar.

MADALENA DO MAR

Madalena do Mar is a coastal village in the municipality of Calheta. Discovered as a surfers' paradise a few years ago, champions from all over the world travel here to play and practise in its waves. This new activity has changed the population's lives in the last ten years, resulting in the building of a hotel and several restaurants. The population is very receptive to the sport, and there are some excellent surfers among its residents.

Traditionally an agricultural area with a considerable banana production exported to the Portuguese mainland, Madalena do Mar is also a fishing region, its closeness to the sea bringing constant contact with and love of this work.

Madalena do Mar is now opening up to new opportunities in the tourism sector, thanks to a new accessibility that has brought it closer to the main towns of neighbouring municipalities.

Interior of Canhas Parish Church.

Bottom: cross dedicated to the Sagrado Coração de Jesus and Santa Terezinha in Canhas parish.

ARCO DA CALHETA

The name Arco da Calheta originates from the particular configuration of mountains that surround the parish, created in 1572, governed from the old São Braz Chapel, which has remained the patron of this population. Arco da Calheta, before it was integrated into the parish of Calheta, now the biggest municipality in Madeira, was one of the first places on the island to use intensive agricultural practices. Since the first colonisers arrived, in the second half of the fifteenth century, conditions have proved adequate for farming, with fertile land and plenty of water. Over the years, many water channels have been built to take water to agricultural areas, the most important of which being Rabaçal and Madre Grande, the latter with its source on the Paúl da Serra plateau.

The parish is also known for its fairs, popular festivities which go on for around a week and attract many people from all over the island, and lately, many emigrants that were born in the parish and who assume responsibility for the organisation of the religious festivals.

As well as the São Braz Festival on 3rd February, there is also the pilgrimage and Loreto Festival on 7th and 8th September.

CANHAS

The parish of Canhas owes its name to the Canha family, which settled there in the early days of colonisation. João de Canha, an arms-bearer for the Duke of Viseu, Dom Diogo, and one of the first settlers in Canhas, had plots of undeveloped land here, having leased them from Dona Constança Rodrigues de Almeida, widow of João Gonçalves Zarco.

This parish, created in 1577, is considered to be an inland area, because it only has a tiny section of coast, there is nevertheless a small port here, named Anjos after the place in which it is located. The place itself takes its name from a chapel built to Nossa Senhora dos Anjos.

The patron here is Nossa Senhora da Piedade (*Our Lady of Mercy*), whose religious festival is held on the first Sunday of August. The parish of Canhas is greatly influenced by the emigrants that built many houses here, and have been responsible for much of the development in the parish over recent years. The island's older rural habits have been preserved, thanks to the parish's inland characteristics. It has a great productive tradition - since last century the parish has housed four factories: a butter factory, a sawmill, a brandy distillery and a pasta factory. In its location between mountains, the parish of Canhas is also situated on the route between various inland settlements to the East of the island, which look to Canhas for supplies. Times and customs have changed, but the population of Canhas is still an important part of the economy of the West coast of Madeira.

CALHETA

Calheta is one of the oldest parishes on the island. It takes its name (*creek*) from a small inlet on the coast. Raised to town status by royal charter in 1825, it was one of the first places in Madeira to industrialise agriculture. Agriculture-based "industry" was important to the municipality's economy; at one time it boasted eight sugar mills, of which only one continues to operate.

The municipality is the largest and westernmost on the island, including the parishes of Prazeres, Calheta, Arco and Estreito da Calheta, Fajã da Ovelha, Jardim do Mar, Paúl do Mar and Ponta do Pargo.

At Paúl do Mar and Jardim do Mar, surfers brave the spectacular waves, regarded as the finest in Europe. There are a number of restaurants in these fishing villages where different fish specialities can be enjoyed.

The parish of Jardim do Mar is a veritable oasis lying between the sea and the mountains. Apart from fish, the parish is rich in agricultural crops because of its excellent soils.

The parish of Prazeres exudes peace and quiet, serenity and charm. From Calheta it is easy to reach the Plateau of Paúl da Serra, leading to Rabaçal. Here, the Madeiran forest is still in its primeval state, clothing the mountains like a green blanket. Rabaçal is a good starting point for some of the most picturesque and impressive walks.

The *Casa das Mudas*, at **Arco da Calheta**, holds exhibitions of sculpture, painting and craftwork portraying, among other themes, ethnographic aspects of the Autonomous Region of Madeira.

Playing cards in Calheta.

Calheta and its picturesque harbor.

JARDIM DO MAR
PRAZERES

In recent years, Jardim do Mar, together with the near-by villages of Madalena do Mar and Paúl do Mar, has become one of the most highly regarded and popular surfing beaches with both Portuguese and foreign young people. Its spectacular waves are regarded as the finest in Europe and Jardim do Mar is constantly featured in surfing magazines. A village in the municipality of Calheta, Jardim do Mar lies on the west coast of Madeira and is a good centre for exploring the local hills and beauty spots. As a fishing village, it has a number of highly sought-after fish restaurants that serve local specialities.

The inhabitants of Jardim do Mar make their living from agriculture, local tourism and remittances from emigrants.

The parish of Prazeres in the same municipality is more mountainous and also mainly agricultural. Gardens are very popular here, and every house, built in a highly individual style alongside the lanes, has its own flower patch. Prazeres (the name means 'Pleasures' in English) is well-named, for its inhabitants have long been devoted to the pleasure of gardening.

Jardim do Mar is nowadays very popular with surfers.

FAJÃ DA OVELHA

Time seems to stand still in Fajã da Ovelha, a parish in the municipality of Calheta where the scale of the landscape and the green of the fields are an invitation to reflection. It lies amidst the mountains, with wide views over the sea from its hilltop farmlands. Until only a few years ago, cars heading for Paúl do Mar passed through the parish, winding their way along the twisting old highway that, some decades ago, provided for the first time a way out of Paúl by land. Until then, its inhabitants had no other choice than to receive their goods by sea and to send the bananas and other fruit they grew along the shore to Funchal in the same boats.

Fewer people pass through Fajã da Ovelha nowadays. The tunnels to the south link connect with the municipal capital and have made communications much easier, and it is only on festive occasions, such as the feast day of its patron saint, São João, that many people are to be seen in the parish. Apart from that, it is an area that suffers from major emigration, particularly to South Africa.

Since it has gained a reputation as a relaxing destination, a small amount of Rural Tourism accommodation has begun to be available. It is an excellent choice for a relaxing break between two driving trips round the island.

Decorations for the Festival of St. John, patron saint of Fajá da Ovelha.

Festa de São João

St. John's Festival in Fajã da Ovelha is the busiest celebration in the Parish. It is the festival of the patron saint, celebrated on 24th June, and sponsored by the locals who have emigrated to find work. This is a typical festival in Madeira, following the same pattern as the other typical summer celebrations that take place throughout the island. St. John is actually a very important saint in Madeira, many churches and chapels having been given this name.

PAÚL DO MAR

Paúl do Mar is one of the Madeira archipelago's most important fishing centres, and the sea has given it an incredible variety of fish, making it a real reference in the world of gastronomy.

Small in size, the parish is set below the escarpment of a sheer mountainside.

Most people born here in the last sixty years have left for foreign parts, mainly Venezuela, South Africa, the United States and Panama, where they work in fishing-related activities, among others. The remaining population is largely dependent on money sent back by these emigrants.

A silent, melancholic and peaceful place, its first hotel with more than fifty rooms is an ideal location to recharge batteries, far from the bustle of the cities. When you leave Paúl do Mar through its long tunnels, you leave behind a paradise.

The nearby Ponta do Pargo lighthouse controls navigation arriving at Madeira from the West.

PONTA DO PARGO

Ponta do Pargo is known as the land of the lighthouse, and is situated on the far West coast of the island. On the top of the furthest protruding rocks, a lighthouse was built, in a place which has always been known as Vigia (*lookout*). The lighthouse was only built in 1922, after the population had complained to the authorities that so many ships had been lost there. Today the lighthouse is automated, as all of the island's lighthouses are.

Lombada dos Marinheiros

Lombada dos Marinheiros is an agricultural area, which gives a wide panoramic view of the hills of Calheta, in the East of the island. It is a pleasant area, quiet and sun-baked. It is near to Prazeres, a parish that produces many flowers along the regional road as it passes through.

The land here, as with most land in the region, is greatly suited to vegetable growing and small pastures for cattle. The population works the land, especially the women and elderly, as the younger men have either emigrated or become involved with civil construction, which is a more profitable activity.

At the top of the rocks, in a flatter area, there is a parish made up of good farming land. The people living here are still as tied to the same customs and traditions as they always have been, and have kept the land for pasture areas and vegetable cultivation, although it is mostly used for cattle rearing and dairy production. Here, as in many of the parishes of Porto Moniz and Calheta, the milk that is collected is used to supply the butter factories, which in the first half of the twentieth century began to be run by private producers, and the butter was often exported to continental Portugal and the rest of Europe in metal packaging. Butter from Madeira has become a renowned European product.

The parish is also rich in water sources to irrigate fields and fill them with nutrients. One of the main rivers is called Vacas (*cows*), due to the cattle grazing nearby. The small patches of agricultural land, known as 'lombadas', are characteristic of this Western region of the island, and are crossed by water channels which carry water to the agricultural fields and fertilise the pasture.

Facing page:
Top, view of Paúl do Mar; bottom, sheer cliffs at
Ponta do Pargo.

Ponta do Pargo lighthouse, the westernmost point of
Madeira.

Making the most of the sun to dry clothes, somewhere in
Ponta do Pargo.

ACHADAS DA CRUZ

Achadas da Cruz is a parish in the municipality of Porto Moniz. It is located between the Pontas (*Capes*) do Pargo and Tristão, protruding rocks which stand out on the Western coast of Madeira. It is a picturesque region, with a small population, which is dedicated to agriculture and handicraft activities. The first inhabitants are thought to have arrived here by land at the beginning of the sixteenth century, many years after the island was first colonised. For many years, this was a point of thoroughfare between the Fanal mountains and Pico da Arruda, which are located deep inland on the island, and are subject to dense winter fogs in the Laurisilva Forest. It was also on the way to Porto Moniz, which is easier to reach by the West coast than the North coast, as the hazardous rocks near Seixal made it difficult to get there by land, only a sea passage was possible.

The parish is around eight kilometres from the municipal capital, Porto Moniz, and about the same distance from Ponta do Pargo. Nowadays, access to Achadas de Cruz is easy, by means of the regional road which passes through the Western area of the island, from Calheta to Porto Moniz. In the heart of the settlement there is a nucleus of houses mainly belonging to emigrant workers or ex-emigrants, who went abroad to seek their fortune. At the beginning of the nineteenth century many locals from the parish set sail for Brazil, where they worked hard and amassed a considerable wealth. More recently, over the last 60 years, the tendency has been to move to South Africa and Venezuela. Many of these emigrants do not forget their homeland, and in Achadas de Cruz, just as in other parishes in Eastern Madeira, you can see many uninhabited villas, belonging to these emigrants who visit home only once in a while.

The people of Achadas de Cruz are more in touch with the mountains than the sea, with which they have little contact. Access by foot is practically impossible, and there is only one very dangerous footpath leading between steep cliffs and agricultural patches. A few years ago a cable car was set up, which swoops down over the cliff edges to several small agricultural fields. The cable car brings products from the land, which are then sold in regional markets. Previously, men had carried them on their backs in small quantities, as they climbed the steep and hazardous paths.

Handicraft work is both an activity and a livelihood for the population of Achadas da Cruz, especially among women and the elderly, who are less suited to working the land, given that the latter requires more physical strength and stamina. Linen (flax) spinning and wickerwork are examples of traditional handicraft activities. Flax growing is being restarted now, through rural extension programmes in mountainous and well-irrigated areas. Achadas da Cruz is located

between two important rivers, Moínhos and Lagos, and is therefore ideal for this type of farming. The same is true of osier plants, which provide the material for wickerwork.

Handicraft activities in Achadas de Cruz benefit from privileged treatment by the Casa do Povo structures, as is happening all over the island, including a community programme to recuperate popular roots and traditions.

Top, road between Achadas da Cruz and Santa.

Worker on her way to work, lunch in her basket.

SANTA

The parish of Santa takes its name from the old chapel built in the sixteenth century dedicated to Santa Maria Madalena. It belongs to the parish of Porto Moniz, which is now the municipal capital, and was one of the first to be built in the North of Madeira.

The chapel has undergone several refurbishments over the centuries, the first of which took place at the end of the eighteenth century. These repairs were necessary because the parish is subject to heavy rain during winter, and is located in an area of dense vegetation, with a very humid climate.

The storms affecting the area made repairs necessary, and the structure of the chapel was improved and enlarged with each refurbishment. There is a famous pilgrimage to this chapel, as well as a cattle fair which soon gained significant size and recognition on the island. This still exists today, albeit with more industrial characteristics.

The *Cattle Fair-Exhibition in Porto Moniz* is now the most important agricultural and cattle rearing event in the Autonomous Region and takes place in the parish of Santa, in a place named Portas da Vila in Porto Moniz.

As an agricultural and cattle rearing region, Santa is one of the only areas on the island to have unfenced fields, especially for its cattle rearing, which has increased to a considerable economic dimension, and which represents a way of life for most of the locals.

PORTO MONIZ

The name Porto Moniz replaced the former Ponta do Tristão in 1533 and was a tribute to Francisco Moniz, who married a grand-daughter of Gonçalves Zarco, to whom the place was donated. The settlement grew around a chapel built by this man to form the modern-day town and one of the oldest parishes in the North of Madeira.

Porto Moniz was isolated from the rest of the island until after World War II, when a road linking Porto Moniz and São Vicente was built. This road was literally dug into the slope and is crossed and covered in some areas by waterfalls making their way down to the sea.

The road snaking along the basaltic slopes of the North of Madeira is considered to be one of the loveliest on the island. Tunnels have been built, making it a secondary road and now less passable, with traffic only permitted in one direction in some places. Until a few years ago, cars and busses travelled in both directions and some postcards of the North of the island still depict this.

The island's most north-westerly point is also one of its most magnificent. Without a doubt, the most panoramic route is the one along the North coast from Santana to Porto Moniz. Today however, the journey to Porto Moniz is much faster, thanks to the building of several tunnels making the link between Funchal

Top, statue of Nossa Senhora dos Bons Caminhos.

The island's natural pools.

View of Port Moniz.

The sea and the natural pools make an impressive sight.

and Porto Moniz around 45 minutes. Previously, it took at least three hours along steep roads.

The town's main attraction is its natural swimming pools formed of volcanic rocks filled by the tides with crystal clear water. Also in Porto Moniz are the parishes of Porto do Moniz, Seixal, Achadas da Cruz and Ribeira da Janela.

A bird's eye view of Ribeira da Janela.

Landscape near Seixal at a tunnel exit.

Seixal fishing port.

RIBEIRA DA JANELA

Ribeira da Janela is one of the most picturesque boroughs in Porto Moniz. A farming region set on the slopes of the Paúl da Serra plateaux, it was largely deserted in the fifties and sixties due to emigration.

It is home to the first of two hydroelectric plants built in the second phase of Madeira's hydroagricultural plan. Completed in 1965, it is powered by water from the slopes of Paúl da Serra above the valley of Ribeira da Janela.

It is the only permanently operating electrical plant by the sea at a river mouth, and the water cannot be re-used for irrigation or for a second production level. The loading chamber is situated over the town of Porto Moniz and the pressure pipeline uses a water drop of nearly 400 metres.

Vital to the North coast's energy supply, the Ribeira da Janela plant is part of the Madeira Electricity company energy system that crosses Paúl da Serra to Calheta.

SEIXAL

The first settlers decided to establish themselves in Seixal in 1567. They arrived by sea, as at that time there was no way of reaching the site by land. The mountains and cliffs were frightening and the forest was wild. The sea was the only route open to people arriving or leaving the settlement.

As the area was populated, its inhabitants began to explore the boundaries of the land and to look for paths through to neighbouring lands. The people of Seixal were isolated for many years, surviving on agriculture and fishing, as the sea and land were full of natural resources. The population only began to grow when better boats were accessible, from the 17th century onwards, and by the 18th century Seixal had a population of around 3,500 inhabitants.

With the arrival of roads and

Serving "poncha" in a Seixal bar.

access tunnels, the parish began to change, but agriculture and fishing are still the dominant factors in the day-to-day life of the population of Seixal.

The story of Seixal is the story of its people. For twenty years the population has not grown, as there has been a generalised trend towards emigration. The locals are searching the world for better living conditions. Nowadays, as they carry a sheaf of herbs on their backs to feed the cow, which is kept near the house and gives milk for the family, and have a "poncha" (*a local drink consisting of sugarcane brandy, lemon juice and honey*) in a nearby bar, inhabitants will await a letter from abroad, as they all have family working overseas. Tourists are very well received in Seixal. It is a region full of tradition, good restaurants and an inn looking out over the gracious quay, where the view spans the vastness of the sea and the daunting face of the rocks to the North of island of Madeira.

A section of the coast near Seixal.

Transporting grass to feed cattle.

View of São Vicente.

View of the fully recovered pedestrian zone in São Vicente.

SÃO VICENTE

The district of São Vicente is situated to the North of the island, in the opposite direction to the city of Funchal, the capital of Madeira. It incorporates the parishes of Boaventura, Ponta Delgada and São Vicente, the latter being the seat of the municipality.

São Vicente became a town in the year 1744, and progressively gained status as the most populous region in the North of Madeira, widely renowned as a wood-producing region.

Although it is unknown exactly when the process of population took place, evidence indicates that by the end of the fifteenth century, Northern peoples were already building the houses and other constructions which graciously adorn this humble and picturesque region.

It was from the eighteenth century onwards, however, that São Vicente gained another socio-economic dimension, in connection with the cultivation of vineyards and sugar cane, wood and the production of lime. São Vicente soon became the most important region in the North of the island.

The natural relief of the land itself facilitated the construction of paths and routes to guarantee access for

people and products. However, it was the important "water route" via the sea, by means of coastal navigation, that effectively guaranteed the exchange of some products to other ports on the island.

Throughout the parishes of this municipality there is an interesting nucleus of rural houses, known locally as manor houses, as they were once inhabited by lordly families. Built in the peak years of the wine industry, the most noteworthy of these houses are the Ladrilho Manor House in Ponta Delgada, a region which became known as the Northern Court, the Boaventura Manor House, in Boaventura, and the Fajã Alta House in São Vicente.

There are already several hotels and good restaurants, which are creating a move towards the service industry amongst the youth. The roads in São Vicente are known from postcards. Cars travel slowly and carefully through narrow roads which look vertiginously out over the sea.

THE CAVES OF SÃO VICENTE

One of the sights worth visiting in the parish of São Vicente is the Caves, which are a real trip to the centre of the earth. These are marks left behind from the last period of volcanic activity, and extend over 700 m underground, allowing visitors to get close to this power which has been dormant for millennia.

Located on the left bank of the São Vicente riverside, in a place known as Pé do Passo, one kilometre from the town. The caves are around 400 thousand years old, volcanic in origin, and made up of a series of tubes of lava.

These are the first of this type of open volcanic cave open to the public in Portugal, after their inauguration on 1st October 1996. They stretch around 700m in length, including three galleries, where visitors can enjoy an extraordinary show of volcanic stalactites, lava flows, lava deposits (known as "lava cakes") and the "wandering block", a piece of stone transported by the lava but which got caught in the inside of one of the tubes due to its size.

Parish Church and Baptismal Font.

Image of São Vicente, the parish's patron saint.

The population is mostly involved in agriculture, which, as with many parishes in the North of the island, is destined for subsistence consumption.

General view of Ponta Delgada.

Capela de Santo António in Ponta Delgada.

PONTA DELGADA

Until the nineteen-forties, the parish of Ponta Delgada was an isolated location in the North of Madeira, its name reflecting its difficult access: people had to walk over two sticks balanced on a rock and the more nervous "lost the sight from their eyes", as recorded by a historian. Hence the name Ponta Delgada (very thin point).

Settlement of the parish took place between 1466 and 1469, acquiring its parish status in 1550.

Ponta Delgada belongs to the municipality of São Vicente, a quiet location producing a quality wine well-known throughout the island. The population lives from agriculture and money sent back by its emigrants.

Built in the sixteenth and eighteenth centuries is the Capela (*Chapel*) do Bom Jesus. The simplicity of its exterior is in marked contrast to the ornate decoration of its interior, which is rich with a clear sense of theatricality. Preserving its grey carved stone doorway, the retable inside boasts three canvasses depicting the Adoration of the Magi (the three wise kings), St. John the Baptist and one of the church's bishops. The altar front imitates patterned fabric.

BOAVENTURA

Boaventura appears to have been founded much later than Ponta Delgada and S. Vicente. However, the fact that the place lies on the road south via Curral das Freiras has undoubtedly contributed to its development. The first recipient of a royal land grant is thought to have been the Castilian Pero Gomes de Galdo, who founded the chapel of St. Christopher here. The correspondence between the present parishes and parish churches in the municipality was only established in 1836 with the foundation of the parish church of Boaventura.

Boaventura parish church was for many years a daughter chapel of the parish church of Ponta Delgada, and it was not until 1733, with the creation of the curacy, that the two were separated, with the Chapel of Santa Quitéria becoming the parish church. The whole of Boaventura's history up to the 19th century has its roots in its subordination to the parish church of Ponta Delgada. It was only in 1872 that the situation changed, when the creation of parish councils made Boaventura independent. The most remarkable fact in all this is that Boaventura had a larger population in the 19th century than Ponta Delgada and yet had to wait many years for its importance to be recognised.

Worker.

View of Boaventura.

FAJÃ DO PENEDO

Fajã do Penedo is a hamlet located in the parish of Boaventura, in the municipality of Santana. It is renowned for its high mountains, which tower over a deep valley running down to the river with the same name. The local church is dedicated to the Immaculate Heart of Mary.

Fajã do Penedo, which is an agricultural area, is sparsely populated. Due to its relief characteristics, the region is hazardous and is subject to frequent landslides. The locals, who live on the agricultural plots common to the whole island, have to keep a watchful eye on any movements of the earth. During the rainy season, the earth is washed down to the bottom of the river, where it is carried along by the winter currents, causing blockages and stormy waters which can have catastrophic effects.

At the end of the seventies, one of the worst landslides to hit the North of the island took place in Fajã do Penedo, killing more than ten people, who were taken by surprise by the river's unusually high flow.

However, these are very productive plots, and the people who farm them dedicate themselves to cattle farming. Fajã do Penedo has very harsh winters, but an extraordinary beauty. On a clear, sunny day, its mountains pay homage to the power of nature, shouldered by their lush ravines.

Most of the population of Fajã do Penedo works in the wine and wicker industries.

ARCO DE SÃO JORGE

The name of the parish of **Arco de São Jorge** (*St. George's Arc*) was inspired by the mountains that surround it in the shape of a basalt arc and because it was separated from the parish of São Jorge in 1676, becoming a parish in its on right on 28th December of that year. The parish church was founded in 1517, although it was attached to the parish of S. Jorge until 1676. It was initially dedicated to **Nossa Senhora da Piedade** (*Our Lady of Mercy*), as a small chapel next to Sítio do Cais. Settlement of the parish began at the end of the 15th or in the first quarter of the 16th century. The land is fertile and planted with vines, although in the past a variety of crops has been grown, ranging from cereals, sugar cane, osiers and grapes to vegetables and fruit. In recent decades, grapes have become the dominant cash crop. Unemployment is a problem among the unqualified. Many inhabitants dissatisfied with the poor job prospects in the parish and its general situation leave to seek better opportunities elsewhere. Recently, some Rural Tourism initiatives have been started which may increase the number of openings for the better qualified. Communications with more developed centres are not the best and public transport is poor. With very few shops in the village, the inhabitants of Arco de São Jorge are forced to do their shopping in the municipality of Santana.

View of Arco de São Jorge.

"Cabanas de São Jorge" hotel development.

SANTANA

The city of Santana is situated on the Northern coast of Madeira, at an altitude of around 312 metres. It is the capital of the municipality bearing the same name, which is made up of six parishes. For many years the island was renowned for the small chapel to **Santa Ana** (*Saint Anne*), which then became the origin of its name.

The municipality, with all its parishes, offers visitors picturesque and amazing landscapes, where the lush green of farming land combines with shapely land characteristics to create marvellous panoramic views of rare beauty. The parishes of Santana always developed around the basis of subsistence agriculture and a small domestic economy.

It was in the Northern region of the island that the first settlement, colonisation and bush clearing took place. The municipality of Santana is the second largest in Madeira, comprising 9,310 hectares of land.

Santana is famous for its thatched houses - gabled rectangular buildings shaped like upside-down Vs, where the thatched roof generally stretches to the floor. The houses are normally two-storied; one ground floor and

Santana Parish Church.

Sheer cliffs characterise the Santana seafront.

Typical thatched roof house at Santana.

Farmer carrying sweet potato vine for cattle.

Inn at Queimadas.

Wicker drying.

Like most parishes in the north of the island, the population of Santana lives mainly from agriculture.

another loft floor; thanks to the stone blocks plastered with rustic masonry work and fluted roofing; and as a testament to agricultural practice on the island, there are the zinc hay barns used for cattle rearing and shapely stone steps or terracing built along the slopes from basaltic stone - an impressive display of space-creation and skill by these island-dwellers.

The Municipal District of Santana was created in 1832 and implemented in 1835. It originally comprised the parishes of Santana, S. Jorge, Arco de São Jorge, Faial, São Roque do Faial and Porto da Cruz. The latter was later removed from the district, becoming part of the municipality of Machico in 1852.

Recently, the municipality has once again become representative of six parishes, as on 15th April 1989, the village of Ilha was granted parish status.

On an economic scale, Santana is active in the public sector, the hotel and tourism industry, trade and small industry, although in terms of population the largest economic activity is still agriculture and cattle rearing. Agricultural activity has become more diverse, supplying other less productive areas of the island. Along the stone benches (terraces) there are hay barns, covered with straw or zinc, which are not used for hay, but for cattle, bred by monoculture as a complement to the rural economy. Santana was granted city status in January 2001, and is therefore considered to be the first city of the new Millennium.

PICO RUIVO AND ACHADA DO TEIXEIRA

The municipality of Santana is a must for any tourist to Madeira. The beauty of its green fields, the richness of its flora and fauna combine to form a scenario of tranquillity and peace so typical of the region.

Santana is also known as the Garden of the North, and there are few houses without a garden. All the year round but especially in spring the flowers delight passers by. These *canteiros*, the name given to these small gardens, are everywhere, demonstrating the huge sensitivity of the people of Santana. Along the cobbled stoned paths, traditional decorative species also abound: box trees and hydrangeas that perfume the air.

The *levadas*, or small irrigation channels, are deeply rooted in the cultural tradition of the people of Madeira and nature lovers, and provide some fascinating walks through typical landscapes, where Laurisilva, laurel, spurge and cornel cherry, abound along the paths.

Further inside Santana can be found the wild beauty of Achada do Teixeira which is frequently covered by mists. A few minutes walk along a well maintained path is the majestic Pico Ruivo, the highest peak on the island, a real feat of Nature and a must for any visitor.

At Pico Ruivo an inn, directly run by government services, provides accommodation for anyone wanting to watch a breathtaking sunrise above the clouds at an altitude of two thousand metres.

View of the Penha d'Águia rock from the fort at Faial; left, Faial Parish Church.

Trout farm in Ribeiro Frio; bottom, Ribeiro Frio chapel.

FAIAL AND RIBEIRO FRIO

Vale da Ribeira do Faial is an area of great beauty. It is dominated by the rugged banks of one of the most important watercourses in the north of the island. People have settled the area all around, building stone houses and farming the fertile soil in the walled terraces on which stand thatched or zinc-roofed sheds where the milking cow is kept, frequently an important part of families' livelihoods. Settlement of the area is thought to have begun between the end of the 15th century and the early years of the 16th. Faial was one of the first parishes to be settled. On the banks of the Ribeira do Faial, close to its mouth, the first sugar cane mills were constructed, together with the houses where the eldest sons lived who worked the land. These houses, many now in ruins, are an important part of Madeira's historical and cultural heritage, recording as they do an important period in the island's history. The mountain of Penha de Águia dominates the parish and divides the municipalities of Machico and Santana. Before reaching Faial, we recommend those travelling from Funchal to the interior of the island to stop off at Ribeiro Frio, with its luxuriant laurissilva vegetation, cool clear waters, and one of the most important trout farms on the island.

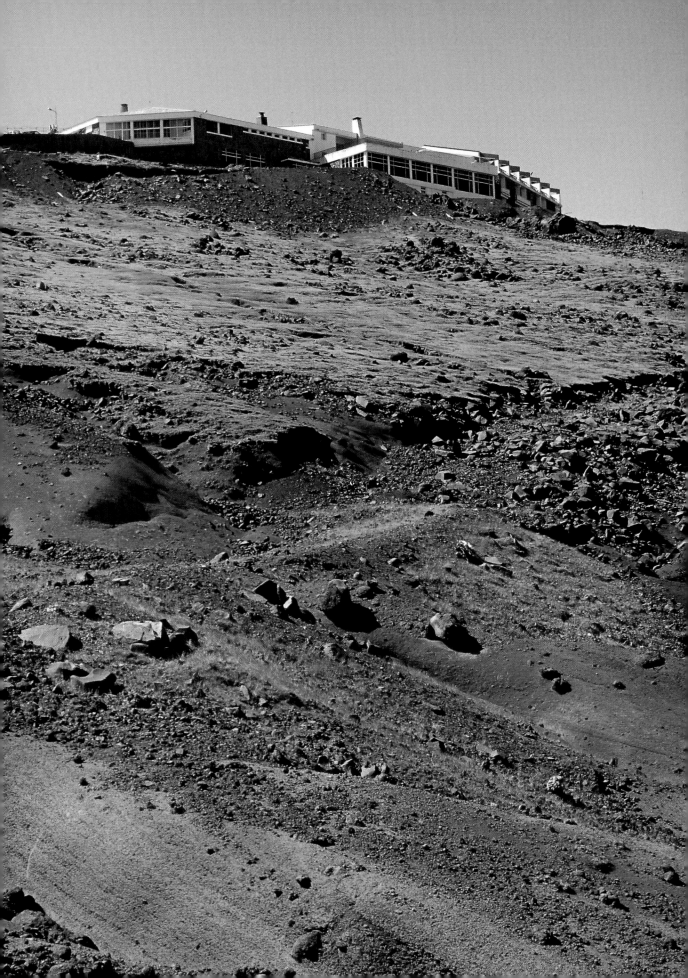

Estalagem (inn) at Pico do Areeiro; top, path between Pico do Areeiro and Pico Ruivo.

PICO DO AREEIRO

Pico do Areeiro, at an altitude of 1818 metres, is one of Madeira's highest peaks. To travel there by car, departing from Funchal, ascend to the parish of Monte passing through Poiso and immediately follow the signposts along the forest road.

At the top of Pico is an inn with a bar, restaurant and accommodation. From the viewpoint behind the inn, a path leads north-east to the top of the mountains, providing an easy route to Pico Ruivo (1862 metres).

Fifteen minutes along the path is the impressive Ninho da Manta viewpoint, whose proud platform affords a view of Fajã da Nogueira, the network of brooks and streams feeding the Ribeira da Metade (River) and be-

yond that the Achadas do Pau Bastião and Cedro Gordo in the parish of São Roque do Faial.

It is a stunning walk with breathtaking landscapes. After the fifth and last tunnel is the path to Pico das Torres. Continuing to Pico Ruivo, the path is signposted, and about half an hour along it is an enchanting wood of timeworn brier bushes sculpted by the wind. In the last stretch before the refuge the path climbs continuously and is the most difficult part of the walk. Walkers can recharge their batteries at the refuge before climbing for a few more minutes to the top of the peak. On a clear day, the view over Curral das Freiras, the valley of the ribeira Grande de São Jorge or the Achadas de Santana is extraordinary.

View of Porto da Cruz; left, Porto da Cruz Parish Church.

Porto da Cruz beach;
bottom, landscape near Porto da Cruz.

PORTO DA CRUZ

In the middle of the last century, Porto da Cruz was known as the land of noblemen, having been settled by entrepreneurs who had become wealthy traders in agricultural production, especially sugar cane, thanks to an important **engenho** (*industrial infrastructure*) that received production from the North of the island. In the first years of the last century there were two more "engenhos" in neighbouring Faial, turning the area into a business centre. The name Porto da Cruz (*Port of the Cross*) was given by the first explorers at the time of colonisation, who, on disembarking on the beach, erected a cross in the little cove that served as port. It was here that the old Leal family lived, owners of one of the island's most opulent manor houses near Capela de S. João Nepomuceno. Porto da Cruz is known for its typical regional wine, commonly known as "American" after the popular table grapes of the same name used to produce it. Every year, a festival is held in Porto da Cruz as a tribute to the Grape and Wine in such a way as to encourage the population and prove the importance of grape-growing to them for the whole parish and Autonomous Region.

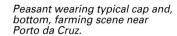

Peasant wearing typical cap and, bottom, farming scene near Porto da Cruz.

PORTO DA CRUZ / PORTELA

The Portela viewpoint between Machico and Porto da Cruz offers a splendid view of the whole parish, with Serra da Penha d'Águia in the background, towering over the sea and flanked at its foot by the villages of Faial, from Porto da Cruz going towards Santana.

The walk from here along safe paths and through beautiful countryside crosses varying types of agricultural land, still mainly cultivated by women, the men having gone on to more profitable professions, e.g. civil construction, or emigrated. After the viewpoint is the path to Cruz da Guarda, which is paved, well maintained and well signposted. From Cruz da Guarda on to Referta, where most farming families keep their cow in a type of byre known on Madeira as "palheiro", a highly profitable monoculture, especially Achada. The alternative by road to Referta manor house is also easy. The descent from Achada to Porto da Cruz is moderate, and the walk is interesting and of little difficulty over nearly ten kilometres and lasting between three and four hours.

Because of the characteristics of the terrain, the route

View of Porto da Cruz and the rock of Penha d'Águia.

for people with underage children. From here you can continue by road or along the parallel levada or small irrigation channels a little lower down, along which there are no abysses between Referta and to or from Porto da Cruz is along a winding road, torn between the mountains that separate Portela from the North of the island. Coming from Machico, the route is through a tunnel, saving a good few kilometres and a lot of time.

Handicrafts and other regional items at the Portela belvedere, which affords a magnificent view over Porto da Cruz.

A moment of rest from cutting grass for cattle.

PORTELA

Portela is a strategic crossing point from the South to the North of Madeira. Going up the Vale da Ribeira de Machico, one of the loveliest places on the island, is Portela and its Viewpoint, which affords a view of the North of the island.

At the Viewpoint, from where visitors can walk along two levadas, or small irrigation channels, through the interior of the island, one will be overwhelmed by the most beautiful countryside. However, for those who wish to continue on foot it is strongly recommended to take a specialised guide or make a thorough study of the available publications before attempting the terrain.

During the day at the Viewpoint, vendors sell regional articles, in particular handicrafts and antiques. Vendors of typical Madeiran and Portuguese regional souvenirs complete the scenario.

The nearby restaurant provides bar service, a cafeteria and light, meals. For the more adventurous, we heartily recommend a walk along the levada to Caniçal at the extreme East of the island.

SANTO DA SERRA

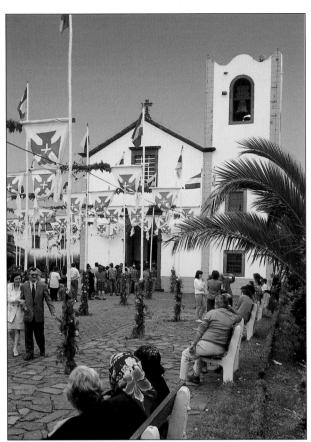

The parish of Santo da Serra is split between two different municipalities. The Eastern half belongs to Machico and the other half is under the administration of Santa Cruz.

It is a charming place, with many tree groves and beautiful villages and farms, many of them built by British subjects living in Madeira at the beginning of the last century. It was here that the first golf course in Madeira was built, with 27 holes, much sought after by both visitors and residents. It has model support facilities in the parish, all of which is inland and surrounded by mountains, which provide excellent landscapes on sunny, clear days, even as far as the neighbouring island of Porto Santo a mere 30 kilometres away.

The Quinta da Junta park, belonging to the Regional Government, is open to the public, and is a mingling ground for the population and tourists, providing a superb view over the Machico Valley. In the park there is a deer reserve as well as well-kept gardens with different flowers in bloom during every season of the year.

Santo da Serra Parish Church.

Deer in Quinta do Santo da Serra.

Local Market

On Saturdays and Sundays several dozen local country folk come together in the main square in Santo da Serra in order to sell the products they grow on their land to the visitors to the market. They also set up food and drink stalls, just like in regional Portuguese festivals. After a disorganised beginning, in which it was difficult to get around the centre of the parish, the local authorities decided to regulate the marketplace, creating a market structure whereby producers interested in displaying their goods could improve their standards of hygiene and their contact with the public.

At weekends in Santo da Serra, the laurel kebab and crumble cake are two specialities of Madeira cuisine that visitors can taste at a local festival, the like of which take place all over the island. Just like in an open market, here everything from potatoes to flowers can be bought at cheaper prices than in the city.

MACHICO

Machico is the place where the discoverers of the island of Madeira, Gonçalves Zarco and Tristão Vaz Teixeira, made their first landfall, in 1419.

According to local legend, however, Robert Machim and his beloved, Ana d'Arfet, had already landed here around a century earlier. Whether or not the legend is true, the fact remains that the name of the municipality seems to be a corruption of the name Machim.

Machico has played a prominent role in the history of Madeira from the beginning, and was one of the first two captaincies on the island. It received its town charter in 1450 and was raised to city status in 1996.

The bay of Machico, together with the deepness of its valley, make it the very picture of natural beauty. Seen from the upper parts of the viewpoint, the valley presents an unforgettable picture, with its patchwork of colours unified by the regularity of the rows of little houses. A working fishing port, Machico is also a popular tourist resort with several top class hotels. The city of Machico is a tranquil place, with excellent hotels and restaurants, and makes an ideal base for walks in the locality. The banks of the stream running through Machico are covered with lush vegetation. In addition to the parish church, places to visit include the 16th century chapel of S. Roque on the old city quay, with its lovely stained glass windows.

A panorama of Machico.

The initial settlement, raised to town status by royal charter in the 15th century, soon became a thriving trading centre. A major market for sugar, wood, wine and other local and foreign products, Machico has developed over the centuries into the nerve centre of the region's economy.

Well diversified economically, Machico is mainly engaged in tourism, construction, services and fishing. Employing a large proportion of the municipality and far beyond it, Machico also benefits

Machico Town Hall.

Gothic style south portal of Machico Parish Church.

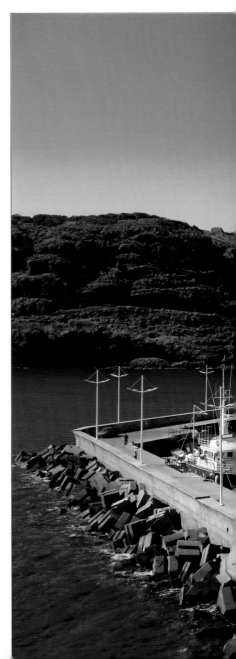

The principal occupations of the municipality are agriculture and fishing. It comprises the parishes of Caniçal, Santo António da Serra, Porto da Cruz, Água de Pena and Machico. The fishing ports are at Machico and Caniçal, and the principal catches brought in there are tuna and bonito.

Caniçal, a well-known fishing town, boasts the only golden sand beach in Madeira. Porto da Cruz, which is mainly agricultural, is famed for its wines and holds an annual wine festival.

The history of Madeira begins in Machico. This inevitably makes it an icon of Portugal's overseas expansion and the archipelago's identity.

from the investment attracted to the area, such as Madeira Airport, Santo da Serra Golf Course and the Caniçal Industrial Duty Free Zone.

The 120-hectare Madeira Free Zone is located in Caniçal, providing suitable facilities for the construction of small factories manufacturing and assembling products for export to European markets.

The parish of Santo António da Serra is home to the oldest golf course in the Region, with 27 holes, and also has a number of beautiful old "quintas", some of them converted into tourist accommodation.

A marina is being built in Caniçal which is expected to attract large numbers of yachts and pleasure craft, making it the prime port of call for sailors in passage from Europe.

Machico.

Machico's picturesque harbour.

CANIÇAL

Caniçal is a small fishing village with a rich religious tradition and one of the oldest parishes in Madeira. It is situated at the eastern end of the island, just before Ponta de São Lourenço, and lies within the municipality of Machico.

On the third weekend in September, the fishermen perform the sea-borne procession of **Nossa Senhora da Piedade** (*Our Lady of Mercy*). The famous festival of the same name also takes place at this time.

Caniçal still makes its livelihood from fishing. It is the base for most of the trawlers that fish for tuna and bonito, fish that are used not only in Madeiran cooking generally (tuna features strongly on Madeiran menus) but also supply the island's canning industry and are exported to Europe and Japan.

Caniçal has the only golden sand beach in Madeira - the **Prainha** (*Little Beach*) - which is very popular with bathers. Famous in earlier times for whaling, the town preserves memorabilia of the industry in a museum that is well worth a visit. The 120-hectare **Zona Franca Industrial da Madeira** (*Madeira Industrial Duty Free Zone*) is located in the parish, housing a number of small factories.

The new **Porto de Mercadorias da Madeira** (*Madeira Cargo Port*) is being constructed at Caniçal, where all cargo for the Autonomous Region will be unloaded, offering the prospect of further jobs. Visitors are recommended to try the many fish restaurants in the town.

Caniçal Wind Farm is a private sector initiative based in the parish and connected to EEM's electricity grid. It has six generators. This renewable energy initiative is regarded as one of the most efficient wind farms in Europe. Constructed in 1992, it is equipped with asynchronous generators installed on 30-metre high towers.

Tuna fishing boat in Caniçal.

Abra Bay in Ponta de São Lourenço Natural Reserve.

Rocky cliff near Caniçal.

Pages 108-109: of all the inlets on Madeira, Abra Bay is the widest, forming an excellent anchorage.

PONTA DE SÃO LOURENÇO

Ponta de São Lourenço is the easternmost peninsula of Madeira, nine kilometres long by two kilometres wide, it includes two small islands (ilhéu *"islet"* da Cevada da Metade or also called Desembarcadouro and ilhéu *"islet"* da Ponta de São Lourenço, also called do Farol or de Fora).

Declared a Natural Reserve in 1982, Ponta de São Lourenço was included in the Madeira Natural Park with the aim of preserving its fauna, flora and geological heritage. Its vegetation is special and unique inside Macaronesia, not because it remains unchanged, but thanks to the presence of important groups virtually confined to this area.

At Ponta de São Lourenço (at the eastern tip of the island), the cliffs tower to 180 metres above the Atlantic in an arid, treeless scenario with only wild flowers sprouting on some sheltered slopes.

The name Ponta de São Lourenço derives from the ship of discoverer Gonçalves Zarco. When approaching it for the first time, Zarco spied the land emerging through the thick fog that was covering the island and which terrified the sailors. Zarco, unable to contain his enthusiasm at the sighting, shouted to his ship: "Oh come São Lourenço!".

The peninsula enters the sea in a succession of peaks, one of them them, behind the bay of Abra, reaching an altitude of 180 m. Of all Madeira's inlets, this bay on the South coast is the largest and the one with the largest recess, forming a good anchorage.

Among the area's fauna are birds, some insects and wild rabbit. There is also an endemic land mollusc, *"Geomitra moniziana"*. The characteristics of Ponta de São Lourenço and all its small bays along the north coast (a large number of caves with interior beaches and very few people) are favourable to the existence of sea lions, an animal commonly sighted in the area. The region's geological constitution is very different from that of the rest of the island, with recently formed volcanic hills of ash and sandstone, sandy-limestone formations in abundance, as recorded in a recent study by the Hydrographic Institute of Portugal.

SANTA CRUZ

Santa Cruz in Madeira is the closest city to the island's International Airport, making it the gateway to the Autonomous Region for visitors arriving by aeroplane. The city is the capital of a municipality made up of four parishes: Caniço, Camacha, Gaula, Santa Cruz and part of Santo António da Serra. The **"Ilhas Desertas"** (*Deserted Islands*), can be seen by those arriving by aeroplane, and also belong to the municipality. The municipality of Santa Cruz stretches from the sea to the mountains, and its people work either in agriculture or services, the latter industry greatly supported by the Airport, which is the source of several hundred jobs.

Madeira Airport now has a 2800 m long runway, allowing for any type of aircraft currently at the service of commercial air companies. There are direct connections to many European cities and an average of fifteen flights per day to Lisbon.

The municipality was founded by Dom Manuel I in 1515, and since then has been renowned for its agriculture and a large area of forest, where many country houses were built over the course of the 19th century for families living in Funchal. Many of these families were British, living in Camacha and Santo António da Serra, which they found to be similar in many ways to their native Britain.

Santa Cruz is a pleasant city with a beautiful seafront promenade, and a park area with terraces, situated between the gardens and the municipal marketplace, where farmers and fishermen sell their products.

Santa Cruz almost certainly owes its name to the first Portuguese seafarers who landed on the island, in the neighbouring town of Machico in 1419. Normally they were accompanied by catholic missionaries, who set up the Cross of Christ wherever they landed. Santa Cruz is homage to their faith and to the fact that they had arrived to a safe harbour. It was given city status in August 1996.

The sunny slopes of Santa Cruz, which are fertile for agriculture, were gradually replaced by residential

In these two pictures, Santa Cruz with the airport in the background.

buildings. Thanks to the tranquillity and the climate, Santa Cruz was chosen as a residence by many hundreds of families working in Funchal. Development in some areas is clearly visible, and the possibility has recently arisen that two parishes, Camacha and Caniço, could soon become the capital of the municipality, given the huge demographic expansion and urban development, consolidated with new amenities and public support services, which have naturally sprung up in these parishes.

Santa Cruz, all in all, has not lost its agricultural traditions. The land is good and fertile. It is sun-drenched and benefits from the water which flows from its mountains and which is carried along *levadas*, or small irrigation channels down to the lowest parts of the municipality. These *levadas* are typical throughout the island, and provide water with which to irrigate agricultural land.

Santa Cruz is also a land of culture. In the very centre of the city there is a permanent exhibition venue, not just for local artists, but also for temporary exhibits of artists from outside the island. Quinta do Revoredo also has accommodation facilities for artists wishing to withdraw to search for inspiration for their works.

The airport of Madera and Santa Cruz seen from Machico. The Airport City, as Santa Cruz is often known, has been subject to complementary growth. Its population is well spread out across the territory, and the city now has to focus on controlling and regulating the growth of hotels and restaurants, in order to preserve the necessary balance.

CANIÇO

Caniço is nowadays one of the most developed parishes in the municipality of Santa Cruz. So developed are parts of its economy that they have led to its elevation from parish to city status.

For the last 30 years or so, Caniço has been popular with tourists and German investors who have built holiday homes here. After a few years, the locals began to follow their example and Caniço is now a dormitory town for people who work in the nearby cities, where they enjoy a good quality of life in detached villas or luxury fenced condominiums.

Because of its closeness to Funchal and its excellent climate all year round, Caniço now boasts the second largest number of hotels in Madeira.

The sun-drenched soils of Caniço are extremely fertile, but agriculture is giving way to building development. Farmlands are being split up into building plots or redeveloped as tourist accommodation. Until recently, the cultivation of onions in Madeira was virtually restricted to this parish. It remains the centre of onion growing but the area under cultivation is now much reduced. At one time, onions were produced in huge quantities, almost all of them for export.

Caniço Parish Church.

Bottom, Caniço Municipal Cemetery

Facing page:
Top, view of one of Caniço's many hotels;
bottom, Garden nooks.

The industry's memory lives on in Caniço's annual onion festival and in a number of cultural, leisure and sporting activities that take place here around this time, at the beginning of the summer.

The cultivation of delicacies continues to be important in Caniço, and a number of families are engaged in this industry in the areas less affected by development.

Recommended places to visit include the **Igreja Paroquial** (*Parish Church*) and the fascinating Quinta Splendida, a hotel in the Italian-Swiss style, set in its own gardens and boasting a restaurant inside an art gallery.

Lettuce growing.

Peasant wearing typical cap near Caniço.

CAMACHA

The parish of Camacha is situated at an altitude of over 700 metres, approximately ten kilometres from Funchal, from which it can be easily reached. It is also on the road between Funchal and Santo da Serra, where Madeira's most important golf course is located.

The name Camacha, according to some books and historical reports, derives from the fact that one of its earliest settlers was called Camacho. On his death, the tenants of his lands were obliged to pay their rents to his widow, who soon came to be called Camacha, the feminine form in Portuguese of her husband's name. The village thus became known by that name and was elevated to parish status in December 1676.

The modern Camacha is highly developed. It has long been traditional farming country, where they still grow osiers which, after cutting and boiling, are made into basketwork and decorative cane items.

With its strong British influence a century ago, it was at Camacha that football was played for the first time in Portugal.

Folklore and ethnographic tradition play an important part in the life of the parish. The Casa do Povo da Camacha Folklore Group, the leading ambassador of traditional song and dance in Madeira, was founded in the parish.

Visitors are recommended to visit the wickerwork factories, a fascinating and varied world where the creativity and craftsmanship of the local men and women is well displayed.

Top, working wicker in Camacha.

Wicker handicraft.

PONTA DO GARAJAU

Ponta do Garajau is an important maritime reference on Madeira's south coast. Forming the boundary of the Bay of Funchal to the east, it is a charming inlet described over many centuries as one of the wonders of the sea-going world. Since the eighteenth century, travel writers, especially British crossing the Atlantic to the West Indies, have often described the entrance to Funchal as fascinating and surprising.

Ships crossing Ponta do Garajau are offered a fine view of the port of Madeira's capital, its calm waters and the old town rising in a beautiful and spectacular amphitheatre and extending along the slopes of Funchal.

The statue of Jesus Christ at Ponta do Garajau, a tribute by the people of Madeira to the cult of the Santíssimo Sacramento, is one of the location's most interesting landmarks and also one of the island's greatest pieces of public sculpture. Inaugurated in 1927 it welcomes visitors from the sea.

Overshadowed by the statue is Garajau Beach, arrived at by car down a winding road. With some hotels just a few hundred metres away, this beach is very popular in the summer with both the local population and tourists.

Garajau and the whole area around Caniço are currently very popular for

Left, statue of Christ at Ponta do Garajau.

people wishing to build villas, and there has been a huge development in real estate in the last few years.

To counter the voracious appetites of real estate developers, who in Madeira aim to live in harmony with a sustained development, the Garajau Partial Natural Reserve was established in 1986. Any construction now planned for the sea strip comes up against the strict recommendations and legislation implied by the existence of a natural reserve. The law which created the Reserve, locates it on the south coast of Madeira at the extreme east of the Bay of Funchal. It is a marine reserve, unique in Portugal, and includes a strip

Garajau Partial Natural Reserve

This reserve, established in 1986, is situated on the south coast of the island, at the eastern end of the bay of Funchal. It is a marine reserve covering a strip between the spring tide high-water mark and a depth of 50 metres.
Among the fauna to be seen here are some of the larger fishes such as the dusky grouper, "*Epinephalus guaza*", along with a wide variety of other coastal species. The reserve is visited annually by schools of giant manta rays, whose size and graceful movements draw visitors from all over the world. All types of fishing are prohibited within the reserve's boundaries. Sailing inside the reserve is also heavily restricted, with only small boats being allowed to beach. Facilities and equipment for deep-sea diving are available.

Garajau beach, a protected area with restricted access.

that extends from the spring tide high-water mark to a depth of 50 metres.
Among the fauna to be seen here are some large fish such as the dusky grouper ("*Epinephalus guaza*"), and a wide variety of other coastal species. Every year, schools of giant manta rays are sighted, their size and graceful movements making the location an international attraction.
All types of fishing in the reserve area is banned. Sailing is also subject to strict conditions, and only small boats going to the beaches are permitted access and mooring.

PORTO SANTO

The island of Porto Santo was discovered in 1418 by the Portuguese João Gonçalves Zarco, Tristão Vaz Teixeira and Bartolomeu Perestrelo, the last later appointed 1st Captain-Donee of the island. The discovery marked the start of the great Epic of the Portuguese Discoveries, begun by Prince Henry. It was named Porto Santo by the navigators, who had found shelter on the island from a great tempest that had been pursuing them.

Also known as **"Ilha Dourada"** (*Golden Island*), by virtue of its long expanse of sand, Porto Santo lies 40 kilometres from the north-eastern coast of Madeira. It has an area of 42.17 square kilometres (11 kilometres long by 6 kilometres wide), and the south coast of the island is coated with a layer of fine golden sand, lapped by the Atlantic Ocean.

Its calm, clear blue sea is the trademark of this increasingly popular holiday destination, with yellow and brown, thanks to its lime soil, its predominant colours. The two islands are linked by boat (a daily ferry transports passengers, cargo and cars, taking around two and a half hours) and by aeroplane, which takes 15 minutes.

The climate is dry and stable, and the temperature varies little from one season to another. It is common to go to the beach all year round, thanks to the pleas-

Portrait of Christopher Columbus and, top left, scene of daily life in the second half of the 15th century.

ant temperature of the sea water, and both air and water temperatures vary between 18° and 22° Centigrade.

Pico do Castelo (438 metres) behind the city boasts a ruined sixteenth century fortress, built for defence.

The Regional Government has set up a forest reserve, which includes a tree planting plan bid to combat soil erosion. The result of this effort is visible on the journey from the airport to the city, with a host of trees and bushes in full flower.

There are hotels along the beach, always fully booked in summer. During the rest of the year, accommodation in the Porto Santo's hotels is easy to find and there is a wide variety of type and quality.

CASA DE COLOMBO (CHRISTOPHER COLUMBUS'S HOUSE)

The presence of the Genoese navigator on the island of Porto Santo is recorded by the Casa Museu de Cristóvão Colombo, which recreates the atmosphere encountered by the explorer on the archipelago when he first travelled there in 1478. He had first gone to Madeira to buy sugar for an important trading house in Genoa and then moved on to the golden island, where he settled. It was here that he married Filipa Moniz Perestrelo, daughter of Bartolomeu Perestrelo,

The magnificent beach of Porto Santo boasts around 8 km of fine golden sand.

Northern Porto Santo.

Bottom, Igreja de Nossa Senhora da Piedade (15th century) and Christopher Columbus Museum House.

by whom he had a son baptised Diogo. After the death of his wife, he returned to Lisbon to present his project for discovering the sea route to India from the West. Christopher Columbus's former house on Porto Santo was fully restored having been a parish residence for many years. Now a museum dedicated to the navigator, among the items on show are not only contemporary furniture, but also engravings by Christopher Columbus, reproductions of costumes of the time and a set of manuscripts, including the log of his third voyage. Many researchers into his work have come to Porto Santo in search of more information on his passage and stay on the island.

During the last few years, this link has also been taken up by the regional authorities, who, with the co-operation of international institutes and European universities, have brought specialists in the field to Porto Santo for seminars and conferences to present, discuss and develop their theses on the navigator's presence on Portuguese territory. This link is now being exploited by tourist promoters and operators to include in holiday programmes of possible interest to North American tourists in the near future. The Columbus route will soon include Porto Santo.

Interior of Parish Church and, top left, panel (17th century) of "Mary Magdalen at Christ's Feet".

Left, Vila Baleira, the small capital of Porto Santo.

Facing page, the marvellous coast of Ilhéu do Baixo.

To give it a new dynamism, the Casa de Colombo is also an open space for exhibitions, conferences or other events in the Arts and Culture area.

In addition to the fame brought to the island by the link to America's discoverer, Porto Santo also possesses some highly interesting works of art in its parish churches, notably a seventeenth century painting of Mary Magdalene at the feet of Christ.

On the cultural side, work has been developed by government bodies to preserve traditions, especially folk music, handicrafts and costume, which due to the island's small size, have gradually been lost over time.

Windmills, an island tradition, are being recovered and are now, as before, an "ex-libris" of the landscape of the golden island.

Porto Santo is currently undergoing huge transformation. Several medium-sized hotels are being planned along the coast, though building by the beach is not permitted. To avoid tourist development affecting the beach, its greatest asset and strength, a minimum distance from the sand has been decreed, and new buildings cannot encroach on land now classified as of maritime domain.

N

Ponta do Tristão
ou da Fazenda *Ilhéu Mole*

Porto Moniz

Santa

Ilhéus da
Ribeira da Janela

Ribeira da
Janela

Achadas da Cruz

Fajã Nova

Fajã da
Parreira

Seixal

Ponta Delgada

Arco d
São Jo

Lombada

Fajã da Areia

Boaventura

Ponta do
Pargo

Ponta do
Pargo

Parque Natural da Madeira

Fajã do Rente

São Vicente

Fajã do Penedo

Lombo

Lombada dos
Marinheiros

Fonte do Bispo

Achada do Cedro

△
1511

Ribeira do Passo

Achada
da Madeira

Ruivo do Paúl

△
1640

**Serra
do Rosário**

Fajã da Ovelha

Rabaçal

Bica da Cana

Casa das
Torrinhas

Paúl do Mar

Prazeres

Boca da
Encumeada

Pico do Furão

Quebrada

Pico Grande

△
1657

Jardim
do Mar

Lombo do Brasil

Casa do
Lombo
do Mouro

Lombo

Curral das Freiras

Estreito da Calheta

Achada
da Calheta

Serra de Água

Chão dos Terreiros

Calheta

Paredes

△
1436

Curral
de Baixo

Arco
da Calheta

Caixas

Jardim da Serra

Madalena
do Mar

Canhas

**Estreito de
Câmara
de Lobos**

Fontainhas

Ponta do Sol

Ribeira Brava

Cabo Girão

**Câmara
de Lobos**

Oceano Atlântico

MADEIRA

Oceano

Baixa do
Meio

Baixa dos
Barbeiros

Ilhéu das
Cenouras

Pico Branco

Pico Juliana
Camacha 447 450 Serra de Dentro

Ponta do
Varadouro Pico do Castelo Pico do Concelho
Barbara Gomes 437 324
227 Serra de Fora

Capela de
Lapeiras Graça

VILA
BALEIRA

Boqueirão de Cima

Ilhéu de
Cima

Pico de Ana Ferreira
283

Ilhéu de
Ferro

Ponta

Boqueirão de Baixo

Oceano

Ilhéu de
Baixo

PORTO SANTO

Oceano

Ponta de São Jorge

São Jorge

beira Funda

Ilha

Santana

Faial

Penha de Águia de Bxo.

Casa das
Queimadas

Penha de Águia

590

Fajã da
Murta

Porto da Cruz

2

Achada
do Teixeira

Achada

Referta

Ruivo

Cruz
da Guarda

do Arieiro

1818

Ribeira
de Machico

Ponta de
São Lourenço

Ribeiro Frio

Parque Natural da Madeira

Caniçal

Santo
da Serra

Esteios

1346

Machico

Monte

Gaula

Camacha

Santa Cruz

Caniço

FUNCHAL

Garajau

Ponta
ta Gorda
ruz

Ponta do Garajau

Oceano

ESPAÑA

Porto

PORTUGAL

Lisboa

980 km

Madeira
(Portugal)

Porto Santo

950 km

Rabat

550 km

MARRUECOS

Islas
Canárias
(España)

ARGÉLIA

MAURITANIA

CONTENTS